LOBSTER'S FAMILY GUIDE TO
NORTH AMERICAN SKI RESORTS

LOBSTER'S FAMILY GUIDE TO

NORTH AMERICAN
SKI RESORTS

MARTY McLENNAN

Lobster Press ™

McLennan, Marty, 1970—
Lobster's Family Guide to North American Ski Resorts
Text copyright © 2001 Lobster Press™
Illustrations copyright © 2001 Lobster Press™

PUBLISHED BY
Lobster Press™

1620 Sherbrooke Street West, Publisher: Alison Fripp
Suites C&D Editor: Alison Fischer
Montréal, Québec Copy Editor: Frances Purslow
Tel. (514) 904-1100 Illustrations: Christine Battuz
Fax (514) 904-1101 Series Design: Zack Taylor Design
www.lobsterpress.com

DISTRIBUTION

In the United States   In Canada
Advanced Global   Raincoast Books
Distribution Services   9050 Shaughnessy Street
5880 Oberlin Drive, Suite 400   Vancouver, BC   V6P 6E5
San Diego, CA   92121

We acknowledge the financial support of the Government
of Canada through the Book Publishing Industry Development
Program (BPIDP) for our publishing activities.

National Library of Canada Cataloguing in Publication Data

McLennan, Marty, 1970-
    Lobster's family guide to North American ski resorts

(Lobster's family vacation series)
Includes index.
ISBN 1-894222-38-5

1. Ski resorts—United States—Guidebooks. 2. Ski resorts—
Canada—Guidebooks. 3. Skis and skiing—United States—
Guidebooks. 4. Skis and skiing—Canada—Guidebooks. 5. Skiing
for children—United States—Guidebooks. 6. Skiing for children—
Canada—Guidebooks. 7. United States—Guidebooks. 8. Canada—
Guidebooks. I. Fischer, Alison, 1977- II. Title. III. Series.

GV854.8.N58M33 2001   796.93'025'73   C2001-900207-6

Printed and Bound in Canada.

Author's Acknowledgment

Although the book is in my name, I couldn't have done it alone. Between my first ski instructor and my tireless editor Alison Fischer, there have been innumerable people that have helped bring this project to fruition.

Without the benefit of several generous corporate sponsors, I could not have researched the book: Air Canada flew us all over the continent; Pontiac supplied us with a new Aztec that served as our home, chariot and office for over six months; Elan put the skis and snowboards on our feet; Columbia Sportswear suited us up in style; Panasonic gave me the Toughbook from which I've produced 100,000 words and counting; Global Star Phones provided the connection so I could warn my editors from remote mountain tops that my texts would be delayed; Pentax and Manfrotto supplied first-rate equipment that I used intensively to cover subsequent stories for *Ski Canada*, *Ski Press* and *Hooked on the Outdoors*. And especially the good folks at Lobster Press™, who supported me every step of the way.

There have also been many silent contributors—including the hundreds of moms, dads and children we interviewed on the road. My good friends Rob and Lesley Sibthorpe-Pahl packed us in the back seat of their minivan with their children Nicola and Eric to experience countless weekend ski adventures. Their effort and input into these pages should not go unnoticed. My immediate family also played a huge role. My mom kindled my love for writing and skiing, while my sister Corinne quit her job to help me research, write and fact check these pages. A big thank you goes out to my longtime ski partner, friend, editor and namesake, Marty Silverstone, and to Bob Kirner, who believed in me.

The most important contributor to this project is my girl-friend and partner—Ruth Mandujano López, who left her home in Mexico and put her life on hold for two years to join me in this adventure. Her endless energy, crucial editing skills and loving support were essential to completing *The Lobster Family Guide to North America Ski Resorts*. This one is for you.

Table of Contents

Author's Introduction

When I was ten years old, winter weekend mornings meant riding in the rumble seat of our beat-up family Pinto, crammed between my brother and sister. Snow or shine, Mom would be behind the wheel, wearing a well-worn, pink one-piece snowsuit. Three of us in the back would be dozing peacefully until a pothole or a quick lane change jolted us from our dreams and we'd ask, "are we there yet?"

Looking out the window today, as we careen across the Sierra Nevada, a quick glance in the mirror reminds me that some twenty years have gone by, but nothing has really changed. We've replaced the jalopy with a shiny red Pontiac. My sister is behind the wheel, while Ruth, my girlfriend and partner sits in the passenger seat. I'm still in the backseat wondering, "are we there yet?" Only this time, I'm surrounded by boxes of research notes, keying in changes to the text on my laptop.

We've spent close to ten months over the past two winters visiting and studying North America's most family-friendly ski resorts. Our passion for the sport has taken us from New England's historic ski towns to the highest lift-accessed terrain in the West. On the way, we've stopped at over a hundred ski resorts. This winter alone, we've driven over 20,000 miles through three mountain ranges, crossed 11 states and two Canadian provinces, and skied 132 days at 65 different resorts. Our goal was to determine the 50 best ski resorts in North America for families.

As the road winds higher up into the mountains, I make a few, final corrections. After two years of research and writing, I can truly say that "yes, we are there." The book you hold in your hand is a testament to our adventure.

Marty McLennan
May 16, 2001
Sierra Nevada, CA

A Word from the Publisher

Lobster Press™ published its first book, *The Lobster Kids' Guide to Exploring Montréal*, in 1998. To date, Lobster has added nine more cities to the series, and the list continues to grow. New this year, we are proud to introduce Lobster's Family Vacation Series. The *Lobster's Family Guide to North American Ski Resorts* will be the first in this series of travel guides geared to vacationing families.

Taking the entire family on a ski vacation can seem like a daunting task, but this book provides a complete resource of valuable information that will allow you to plan an enjoyable, relaxing holiday. Not only does this guide provide practical facts about each resort, but is packed with suggestions for families, on and off the slope.

In 2000-2001, Marty McLennan visited all the resorts listed in this guide, and all the information provided in this book has been verified. However, since prices and business hours are subject to change, call ahead to avoid disappointment. Please accept our apologies in advance for any inconveniences you may encounter.

Prices in this guide are listed in American dollars (US) for sites in the United States and Canadian dollars (CDN) for the ski resorts in Canada. Please refer to our Skiing and Safety Tips section for a conversion of units table and other important information about skiing with children.

One last word: Please be careful when you and your children visit the sites listed in this guide. Neither Lobster Press™ nor the author can be held responsible for any accidents that might occur.

Enjoy! And watch for other books in Lobster's Family Vacation Series. Coming in 2003: *Lobster's Family Guide to Cruises*.

—From the gang at Lobster Press™

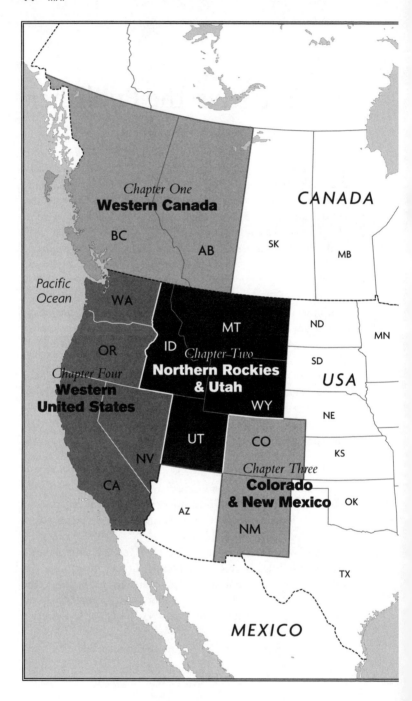

Chapter One
Western Canada

CANADA

BC

AB

SK

MB

Pacific
Ocean

WA

MT

ND

MN

OR

ID

Chapter Two
**Northern Rockies
& Utah**

SD

USA

Chapter Four
**Western
United States**

WY

NE

UT

CO

KS

NV

Chapter Three
**Colorado
& New Mexico**

OK

CA

AZ

NM

TX

MEXICO

MAP **15**

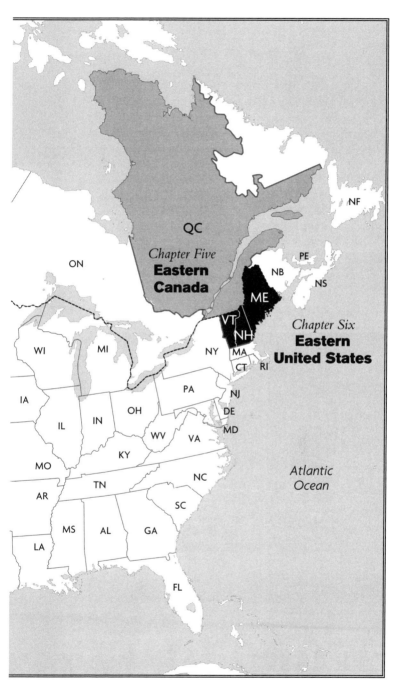

QC

Chapter Five
**Eastern
Canada**

ON

NF

PE

NB

NS

ME

VT

NH

Chapter Six
**Eastern
United States**

NY

MA

CT

RI

WI

MI

IA

PA

NJ

DE

IL

IN

OH

WV

VA

MD

MO

KY

NC

AR

TN

*Atlantic
Ocean*

SC

MS

AL

GA

LA

FL

Skiing and Safety Tips

Once you've decided on a ski resort, be sure to take time to do a little preparation for your trip. Traveling with kids isn't always easy but there are things you can do to ensure your family has a safe, fun trip without any mishaps. These helpful suggestions will help make your ski vacation pleasant for everyone.

- Call ahead to verify the resort's hours, lift ticket prices and special deals. (Please note that all lift ticket prices given in this guide are for full-day tickets).

- If possible, reserve daycare and ski lessons ahead of time.

- If you are traveling across the border, be aware of the currency conversion. Changing your money at a resort is usually more expensive than at your bank back home. Visit www.xe.com/ucc for up-to-date information about exchange rates.

- Pack plenty of layers for everyone in the family. Polypropylene and other fabrics that wick moisture away from the skin make excellent base layers under snowsuits.

- Be sure to bring goggles or sunglasses because snow reflects the sun and can damage your eyes easily. Also be sure to wear sunscreen even on cloudy days.

- Bring toys, games and favorite family videos so that your hotel room or condo feels more like home.

- While out on the slopes, keep an eye out for signs of frostbite (blanched skin) and seek medical attention immediately if anyone appears to be suffering from frostbite.

- This book uses the Imperial system, where distance is measured in miles, height in feet and area in acres. Temperature is measured in Fahrenheit. For those unfamiliar with these units:

    - one kilometer is just over half a mile (0.62 miles).
    - there are about 30 centimeters in one foot (0.98 feet).
    - one hectare is approximately the same area as two and a half acres (2.47 acres).
    - Water freezes at 0°C (32°F). Be sure to bundle up when it's below zero (-15°C is 5°F).
    - Visit www.webcom.com/~legacysy/convert2/unitconvertIE.html for help converting units.

Skier's and Snowboarder's Responsibility Code

1. Always stay in control, and be able to stop or avoid other people or objects.

2. People ahead of you have the right of way. It is your responsibility to avoid them.

3. You must not stop where you obstruct a trail, or are not visible from above.

4. Whenever starting downhill or merging into a trail, look uphill and yield to others.

5. Always use devices to help prevent runaway equipment (such as ski brakes on bindings, and "leashes" on snowboards and telemark skis).

6. Observe all posted signs and warnings. Keep off closed trails and out of closed areas.

7. Prior to using any lift, you must have the knowledge and ability to load, ride and unload safely.

**KNOW THE CODE.
IT'S YOUR RESPONSIBILITY.**

This is a partial list. Be safety conscious.

National Ski Areas Association (www.nsaa.org)

Altitude Sickness

Altitude sickness generally affects people traveling over 8,000 feet but it can occur as low as 6,000 feet. Some children (and adults) contract altitude sickness upon arriving at high altitude areas. Others may not experience it immediately, or may not feel the affects at all. Altitude sickness often lasts only one to two days and is usually preventable if the rate of ascent is slow. Excellent physical condition doesn't affect one's ability to acclimatize to altitude.

Common symptoms include bloating, gas, little or no appetite, dehydration, vomiting and general crankiness. While these may sound like symptoms for other illnesses, as long as these symptoms aren't accompanied by a fever, it's likely that you are suffering from altitude sickness. If symptoms become severe or don't improve after a few days, seek medical attention immediately.

How to acclimatize to altitude:

- Stay a night or two at a lower elevation (under 6,000 feet). This will help speed acclimatization.

- Take it easy. Many skiers can't resist the urge to overdo it the first day or two. Stop when you start to feel fatigue.

- Eat a carbohydrate-rich diet (grains, pastas, fruit and veggies) and reduce fat intake.

- Drink plenty of fluids and more water than usual.

- Avoid salty foods.

- Avoid alcohol, tranquilizers and sleeping pills. All of these slow your body's ability to adjust to change in elevation.

- If necessary, Acetazolamide (Diamox)™ is a prescription drug which can help with acclimatization. Like all drugs, it has side effects and is not for everyone. Seek your physician's advice before using.

CHAPTER ONE

Western Canada

The mountains of Western Canada boast some of the best skiing and facilities on the continent. The resorts in the jagged Rocky Mountains serve up plenty of snowy options for families looking for a winter vacation. From double black diamond bowl skiing to cheap, Canadian prices, visitors to the region won't be disappointed. Just don't expect to ski all the resorts in one trip! Distances between them are large.

Whistler-Blackcomb, just north of Vancouver, has long been considered one of North America's premier ski resorts. Its world-class terrain come with an unparalleled village full of amenities and lodging opportunities. Families looking for smaller, less crowded mountains, desert dry snow and excellent kid's programming should ski the Okanagan region's Big White, Silverstar and Sun Peaks.

For the quintessential Canadian Rocky Mountain experience, visit Banff and its Tri-area resorts (Banff Mount Norquay, Lake Louise and Sunshine Village). Buy an all-inclusive lift-and-transport pass to access superb carving, bowl skiing, some of the best views and après-ski at all three mountains. Those looking for a classic-styled ski resort with friendly locals and snaking fall lines should plan a trip to Kimberley Alpine Resort in the Kootenays. Powder hounds who love bowl skiing (without the crowds) should head to the up-and-coming Fernie Alpine Resort. Each offers competitive children's programming and instruction.

Canadian hospitality is hard to beat and dining options can be exquisite, especially in Whistler and Banff. Families with young children benefit from cheap lift passes, ski lessons and lodging. International visitors can expect great vertical without high-altitude prices. Just make sure to pack warm clothing and games for when the mercury plummets. For best flight schedules and competitive prices call Air Canada (888-247-2262) or visit their web site at www.aircanada.ca. Air Canada and its regional partners offer more non-stop flights to Canadian cities than all other carriers combined.

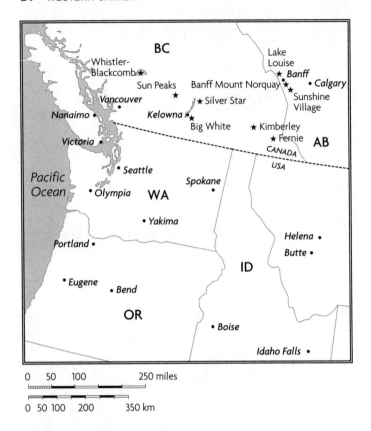

Western Canada

Banff Area
★ Banff Mount Norquay
★ Lake Louise
★ Sunshine Village

Kootenay
★ Fernie
★ Kimberley

Okanagan
★ Big White
★ Silver Star
★ Sun Peaks

West Coast
★ Whistler–Blackcomb

BANFF AREA

Banff Mount Norquay

Less than a ten-minute drive from the center of Banff, Mount Norquay offers a little something for everyone, from chalet bunnies to mogul maniacs. This family-friendly resort has excellent daycare facilities, as well as a terrain park for snowboarders, plenty of groomed intermediate level runs and daring fall line skiing for the experts in your crew. Mount Norquay's small-scale resort makes skiing here a pleasant and relaxing experience.

Well-planned facilities at this mountain include a drop off area where parents can get their kids organized for ski school, pick up a coffee, or grab a bite in the 24,000 square-foot lodge. The lodge boasts two restaurants, a coffee shop and lots of space to store anything you may have brought along, including your lunch. For a nominal fee, you can place your belongings in a personalized basket for safekeeping.

On the slopes, kids and beginners can learn the ropes just outside the lodge by the magic carpet lift, where a self-contained learning area exists. If your family wants to test out the terrain park or venture down other beginner trails, ride the Cascade chair. Intermediate skiers traverse to the Spirit and Pathfinder chairs to enjoy groomed runs. Experts will want to make a beeline for the North American fixed quad chair, where the mountain's black diamond trails are located.

As the smallest of the Banff Tri-areas (Lake Louise, Sunshine and Banff Mount Norquay), bite-sized Mount Norquay appeals to beginners and families with young children who want to ski

BANFF MOUNT NORQUAY
CENTRAL LINE   403-762-4421
CENTRAL RESERVATION LINE   877-762-2281
SNOW REPORT   403-760-7704
ANNUAL SNOWFALL   120 inches.
INFORMATION   www.banffnorquay.com
SEASON   Early Dec−mid-April.
HOURS   Daily, 8:30 am−4 pm   (Fri until 9 pm).

on their own. It is the only resort in the area that offers ski-by-the-hour rates. To make the most of your visit, plan to stay at the Timberline Inn (877-762-2281) and at the end of the day, ski right to the Inn's front door.

👁 At a Glance

ADDRESS Box 219, Suite 7000 Banff, AB T0L 0C0.
LOCATION 1 hour west of Calgary.
TERRAIN MIX 1 mountain, 190 acres.
VERTICAL 2,300 feet (**PEAK** 7,930 feet. **BASE** 5,630 feet).
TRAILS 28 (20% Beginner, 36% Advanced, 44% Expert).
LIFTS 6 (2 quads, 1 high-speed quad, 1 double, 1 magic carpet).
DAILY LIFT TICKETS RATES (CDN) Adults $42, seniors, youths (13 to 17) and
students (18 to 24) with ID $34, children (6 to 12) $15, under 6 free.
NIGHT SKIING TICKET RATES (CDN) Adults $21, seniors, youths (13 to 17) and
students (18 to 24) $20, children (6 to 12) $11, under 6 free.
NIGHT SKIING Cascade Quad and Sundance Conveyor lift (358 feet vertical).
SNOWMAKING 90%.
ACTIVITIES Rent your own hill (private evenings for groups of 50 or more).
BABYSITTERS None.
DAYCARE Kid's Place, daily, 9 am—4 pm. Call 403-760-7709.
CHILDREN'S LESSONS AND CAMPS Snow Sports Center (403-760-7716) or
www.banffskischool.com
HOSPITAL Banff Mineral Springs Hospital (403-762-2222).
SPECIAL DEALS By-the-hour rates, Banff Tri-area ski package ($56 including
transportation).
GOOD MEETING PLACES Cascade Lodge.
GETTING AROUND Banff area shuttle service.
DISTANCE IN MILES Banff, AB 1; Calgary, AB 80; Vancouver, BC 520.

Lake Louise

Situated in the heart of picture postcard Canada, Lake Louise boasts more than just fabulous views. It shoulders some of the best steeps, powder, terrain parks, half pipes and hospitality in North America. And that's not all. From snowboard lessons to backcountry skiing to lounging around at one of the many lodges on the mountain, people of all skiing abilities will find something to love about Lake Louise. Throw in great facilities, reasonable rates and stunning vistas, and you have a prime destination package for families.

When you arrive, you'll want to check out the 36,000 square-foot Lodge of the Ten Peaks. Made from mountain timber, the building has a variety of bars, restaurants, cafés and cozy fireplaces to sit around. Downstairs at the Whisky Jack annex, you'll find guest services, ski school, a small café, lockers and the basket room where you can leave your bag lunches for under $2 per day. If you like a hearty breakfast, stop in at the Northface Restaurant for the best buffet in ski country at only $5.50 a person.

The resort's handy ten-minute parking makes it easy for parents to drop off their kids at daycare or check them into their 9:30 am ski lesson. Adult lessons start one hour later, so frazzled moms and dads can find parking, have a coffee and catch their breath before hitting the slopes. If it's your first time, don't miss the ski school's Discover Program. At $29 for children and $39 for adults, this package comes complete with lift ticket, ski rental and half-day lesson. It's a real deal and a great way to learn to ski.

LAKE LOUISE
CENTRAL LINE
800-258-SNOW (7669) or 403-522-3555
CENTRAL RESERVATION LINE
800-258-SNOW (7669)
SNOW REPORT
800-258-SNOW (7669) or 403-244-6665
ANNUAL SNOWFALL
161 inches.
INFORMATION
www.skilouise.com
SEASON
Early Nov—early May.
HOURS
Daily, 9 am—4 pm.

For skiers big on powder, sign up for First Tracks. Get an hour and a half lesson that starts 30 minutes before the ski lifts open to the public. Or, if you'd rather pick up some free tips and good conversation, meet with the Lake Louise Ski Friends for a complimentary tour of the mountain. Look for the green-jacketed volunteers in front of Beavertails Gazebo every day at 9:30 am and 10:15 am, and also at 1:15 pm.

Beginners heading out on their own should start at the Sunny T-bar. Located in front of the Telus/Chocolate Moose Daycare Center (403-522-3555), the T-bar provides access to gentle slopes and wide-open terrain, perfect for learning. More experienced skiers head up the Friendly Giant or the Glacier Express chairs. While each of the mountain's quads has an easy way down, beginners should avoid the Top of the World Express and the Summit platter. Their steep pitches offer a taste of the resort's adrenaline-packed back bowls. Expert skiers will want to visit the Larch and Summit platter area early in the day. The 40:60 ratio of above the tree line and tree skiing means panoramic views and bowl skiing on sunny days and on less beautiful days, cut trails offer protection from flat light and cold winds.

No matter which lift you choose, plan to meet for lunch at the Whitehorn Lodge. Situated mid-mountain, the facility serves up good food with stunning views of the Rockies from its expansive deck. You can even see the famous Chateau Lake Louise tucked away in the distance. For $49 a person, night owls can partake in bi-weekly torchlight dinners at Whitehorn by riding the Friendly Giant lift up to the chalet just before the 4 pm closing time. Between 4 pm and 8:30 pm, guests will be treated to an unforgettable dinner buffet with live entertainment and dancing. Skiers then don miner's headlamps and descend to the base. Non-skiers ride down on snowmobiles.

If rustic is more your style, call (403-522-3555) and reserve a spot at the famed Skoki Lodge. A seven-mile Nordic ski from Lake Louise's Temple Lodge, guests stay in small, electricity-free cabins and backcountry ski to their heart's content. You'll get two hot meals a day, plus the staff packs lunches for overnight guests.

Families looking for friendly accommodations have a wide variety of options. Located across the highway from the resort, the village of Lake Louise has several reasonably priced places to stay, including the Canadian Alpine Center and International Hostel (403-522-2200). Adults are $25 per night, youths (6 to 12) are $12.50, and those under five stay free. Families can also check out the West Louise Lodge (250-343-6311), about 15 minutes from the ski hill on the Trans-Canada Highway. This hotel offers some of the area's lowest prices, with breakfast included. For those who want top-quality service and amenities, book a room at Chateau Lake Louise (403-522-3511). Its location on the lake is reason enough to spend a night or two.

For families planning to spend a week or more, stay in or near Banff, which has cheaper gas, groceries and amenities than the village at Lake Louise. In Canmore, 20 minutes east of Banff, the Akai Motel (403-678-4664) has excellent prices, from $50 to $90 a night for rooms with cooking facilities. Staying in Banff also makes it easier to get in on the action at the Tri-area ski resorts. Pay $56 a day for lift ticket and bus transportation. The buses, which run daily from 7 am to 5:30 pm, will pick you up and drop you off at your hotel. It's a hassle-free way to ski all three mountains (Banff Mount Norquay, Sunshine and Lake Louise).

👁 At a Glance

ADDRESS   Box 5, Lake Louise, AB T0L 1E0.

LOCATION   2 hours west of Calgary.

TERRAIN MIX   4 faces on 3 mountains, 4,200 acres.

VERTICAL   3,365 feet (**PEAK** 8,765 feet. **BASE** 5,400 feet).

TRAILS   113 (25% Beginner, 45% Advanced, 30% Expert).

LIFTS   11 (4 high-speed quads, 1 triple, 2 doubles, 2 surface tows, 1 magic carpet).

DAILY LIFT TICKETS RATES (CDN)   Adults $54, seniors (over 64), youths (13 to 17) and students (under 26) $43, children (6 to 12) $16, under 6 free.

SNOWMAKING   40%.

NIGHT SKIING   None.

ACTIVITIES   Torchlight Parade, heli-skiing, Nordic skiing, dog sledding, ice-skating, sleigh rides.

BABYSITTERS   None.

DAYCARE   Telus/Chocolate Moose Daycare Center (18 days to 5 years) (403-522-3555).

CHILDREN'S LESSONS AND CAMPS   Kinderski (3 to 4), Kid Ski (5 to 11), Shreddies (7 to 12), Kids Discover Program (403-522-1333).

HOSPITAL   Mineral Hot Springs Hospital (403-762-2222).

SPECIAL DEALS   Banff Tri-area ski package ($56 per day including transportation). Pay $54 for Lake Louise Plus Card and receive discounts at all Resorts of the Canadian Rockies, plus dining and lodging discounts in Lake Louise and Banff.

SPECIAL PROGRAMS   Beyond the Boundary, First Tracks, clinics for advanced skiers and boarders, group lessons.

GOOD MEETING PLACE   Great Bear Room in Lodge of the Ten Peaks.

GETTING AROUND   Lake Louise Ski Area Express, daily, 8 am — 6:30 pm, free.

DISTANCES IN MILES   Banff, AB 36; Calgary, AB 115; Spokane, WA 390; Vancouver, BC 520.

Sunshine Village

For kids, Sunshine Village is the real deal. After all, there aren't many ski resorts that boast a 20-minute gondola ride just to get to the base of the mountain. Its isolated locale and incredible vistas make Sunshine a great destination for families who want to get away from it all.

When you arrive, back your car into the hotel check-in and your bags will be tagged, loaded and in your room within minutes. The ride up can be chilly, so make use of the change rooms at the base of the gondola to bundle up. Then climb aboard and get whisked past pristine wilderness, up to the resort Village. A conglomeration of base lodge, hotel, daycare, restaurants, stores and staff accommodations—the Village center is dominated by one of ski country's largest hot tubs.

The modest but cozy accommodations serve up slope and creekside views and offer guests an excellent family games room that contains Foosball™, free Internet access, pool table, large screen TV and small library. Upstairs, you can either dine dressy or casual at one of the resort's two restaurants. Or, head across the way to the famed Trapper's Cabin for a sampling of local brews and stews.

SUNSHINE VILLAGE
CENTRAL LINE 87-SKI-BANFF (877-542-2633)
CENTRAL RESERVATION LINE 87-SKI-BANFF (877-542-2633)
SNOW REPORT 403-277-7669
ANNUAL SNOWFALL 410 inches.
INFORMATION www.skibanff.com
SEASON Early Nov—late May.
HOURS Daily, 8 am—4:30 pm. *Last gondola up to resort:* Mon—Thu, 5:30 pm; Fri—Sat, 10:30 pm; Sun, 7 pm.

Once you're ready to hit the slopes, be sure to take advantage of Sunshine's lessons and daycare service, available at an exceptional value. Bring your youngsters to the Kids' Kampus and Tiny Tigers Daycare (877-542-2633), housed just below the gondola station. They have a protected slope all to themselves, serviced by a magic carpet lift. There are stuffed mats and pylons covering the trail so beginners can learn to turn easily and without injury. A new ski school and daycare facility is slated to be built at the gondola mid-station in the coming years.

Advanced skiers and snowboarders will love the fall lines on Goat's Eye Peak. Or, head to the Continental Divide chair for great photo opportunities and a chance to ski in both Eastern and Western watersheds (part of the mountain is located in British Columbia). If you're into more of a challenge, ski the unbelievably steep Delirium Dive. You'll need to bring your own transceiver or you'll be refused entry to this run.

The future for Sunshine looks bright, as the resort has planned several projects over the next few years. It may not be as glamorous or as chock-full of après-ski activities as other mountains in the Canadian Rockies, but Sunshine's friendly staff and wonderful setting guarantees your family will feel right at home.

◉ At a Glance

ADDRESS   Box 1510, Banff, AB T0L 0C0.

LOCATION   10 miles west of Banff.

TERRAIN MIX   3 mountains, 3,168 acres.

VERTICAL   3,514 feet (**PEAK** 8,954 feet. **BASE** 5,440 feet).

TRAILS   91 (22% Beginner, 31% Advanced, 47% Expert).

LIFTS   12 (1 high-speed 6-person gondola, 3 high-speed quads, 1 triple, 3 doubles, 2 surface, 2 beginner tows).

DAILY LIFT TICKETS RATES (CDN)   Adults $37, seniors (over 64), youths (13 to 17) and students (18 to 24) $29, children (6 to 12) $11, under 6 free.

SNOWMAKING   0%.

NIGHT SKIING   None.

ACTIVITIES   Family nights at the Sunshine Inn.

BABYSITTERS   Tiny Tiger Daycare (877-542-2633).

DAYCARE   Tiny Tiger Daycare, daily, 8:30 am—4:30 pm, 19 months to 6 years (877-542-2633).

CHILDREN'S LESSONS AND CAMPS   403-762-6560.

HOSPITAL   Mineral Hot Springs Hospital (403-762-2222).

SPECIAL DEALS   Check www.skibanff.com for seasonal specials. Banff Tri-area ski package ($56 including transportation).

GOOD MEETING PLACES   Sunshine Inn (base), day lodge (base).

GETTING AROUND   Banff Tri-area shuttle service runs all day.

DISTANCES IN MILES   Banff, AB 10; Calgary, AB 84; Vancouver, BC 520.

KOOTENAY

Fernie

The secret is out! Fernie's spectacular alpine hideaway has suddenly become a haven for powder hounds. Since Resorts of the Canadian Rockies bought the mountain in 1997, Fernie has doubled in acreage and transformed itself from a fledgling resort to an international ski Mecca. The reasons are simple. Fernie boasts the largest snowfall in the northern Rockies, a relatively warm climate, an expanded base facility and some of Canada's best bowl skiing. The fact that the resort is situated in a picturesque mining town is icing on the cake.

Located four hours south of Calgary's international airport, Fernie's temperatures are decidedly warmer than most western Canadian resorts. This is a big bonus for kids, whose little fingers and toes get cold easily. Also, the majority of the ski crowd heads north to Banff, so you'll likely find yourself in the company of other value-seeking families.

Tykes in your troop? Drop them off at the Resorts of the Canadian Rockies signature daycare or ski school. The resort offers a variety of lessons for all ages, from skiing to snowboarding to telemarking. If you'd like to carve in fresh powder, pay $33 to join the First Tracks program and start skiing an hour before the lifts open to the public. First timers get excellent value with Fernie's Discover Skiing program. The special includes a lift ticket, equipment rental and group lesson for $42.

FERNIE ALPINE RESORT
CENTRAL LINE 800-258-SNOW (7669) or 250-423-4655
CENTRAL RESERVATION LINE 800-258-SNOW (7669)
SNOW REPORT 250-423-3555
ANNUAL SNOWFALL 350 inches.
INFORMATION www.skifernie.com
SEASON Mid-Nov—late April.
HOURS Daily, 9 am—4 pm.

As Canada's fourth largest resort, Fernie offers trails for every ability, whether it's packed, groomed or loose powder. Near the base, a plethora of easy runs for new skiers are serviced by the

Mini Moose and Mighty Moose surface lifts. Intermediates can venture up the Deer and Elk chairs while advanced skiers test their talents on the mid-mountain blue trails. For those black diamond thrills, experts can ride any of the uppermost lifts to reach the expansive open bowls. Snowboarders need not worry. There's a terrain park especially for them and lots of natural hits.

For après-ski activity, families love to wander through the village, pop into one of the local restaurants, or partake in the entertainment offered in the evenings. Kids can join the Evening Snow Club that runs daily from 6 pm to 8 pm and costs $15. Activities include tobogganing, arts and crafts, and a visit to the local horse barn. There are also weekly talks and slide shows on a variety of mountain themes, including avalanches and skier safety.

If you're getting together for lunch, check out the Lizard Creek Lodge (877-228-1948), one of the resort's on-slope luxury hotels. A gourmet meal will run you less than $10. The accommodations and amenities at this Lodge are some of the best around, so consider staying a night or two. At Fernie, families get a great deal — the food is good, the skiing is top-notch, and there are plenty of activities to keep the little ones amused. And the best part? It all comes at affordable, Canadian prices.

👁 At a Glance

ADDRESS 5339 Ski Hill Rd., Fernie, BC V0B 1M6.
LOCATION Southeastern British Columbia.
TERRAIN MIX 4 mountain peaks, 2,504 acres.
VERTICAL 2,816 feet (**PEAK** 6,316 feet. **BASE** 3,500 feet).
TRAILS 106 trails and 5 alpine bowls (30% Beginner, 40% Intermediate, 30% Expert).
LIFTS 10 (3 high-speed quads, 2 triples, 4 surface, 1 magic carpet).
DAILY LIFT TICKETS RATES (CDN) Adults $54, seniors (over 64), youths (13 to 24) and college students with ID $43, children (6 to 12) $15, under 6 free.
SNOWMAKING 1%.
NIGHT SKIING None.
ACTIVITIES Torchlight Run and BBQ, Activity Knights (barn visits, games, tobogganing), sleigh rides, snowmobile tours, Nordic skiing, snowshoeing, dog sledding, spa, ice fishing.
BABYSITTERS 800-258-SNOW (7669).
DAYCARE Fernie Alpine Resort Daycare (250-423-4655).
CHILDREN'S LESSONS AND CAMPS Contact Fernie Alpine Resort Winter Sports School at 800-258-SNOW (7669).
HOSPITAL Fernie District Hospital (250-423-4453).

SPECIAL DEALS   Multi-day lift passes (3 days or more): Adults $50 per day, seniors and students $38 per day. One-month pass: $499 + tax. Fernie and Kimberley tickets are transferable.

SPECIAL PROGRAMS   The Ultimate Edge ski/snowboard weeks include morning lessons, NASTAR race, video analysis and après-ski reception. First Tracks, Turn and Burn, and other specialty afternoon clinics for advanced carvers.

GOOD MEETING PLACES   Day Lodge Cafeteria (base), The Bear's Den (mid-mountain).

DISTANCES IN MILES   Calgary, AB 188; Cranbrook, BC 62 (airport); Kalispell, MT 116; Spokane, WA 252; Vancouver, BC 594.

Kimberley

Perched at the southern tip of the Purcell mountain range, British Columbia's Kimberley resort has been a family favorite since it opened 30 years ago. Although it tops out at 6,500 feet, visitors still feel they are skiing in the big leagues, since Kimberley is completely surrounded by the majestic Rockies.

A local's hill at heart, the Resorts of the Canadian Rockies bought Kimberley in 1998 and turned it into a world-class ski destination. For a trip down memory lane, bring the kids' box lunches up to the North Star Center and Cafeteria at the upper base. The building's huge glass wall overlooks a small skating pond and offers excellent slope-side views. When the sun is shining, dine out on the deck. If modern is more your style, stick to the lower base where the beautiful Trickle Creek Residence Inn by Marriott (877-282-1200) serves up spacious rooms, gourmet breakfasts and an outdoor hot tub and pool area (wheelchair accessible) that overlooks the beginner-only terrain. Haggard parents can relax poolside while their tots make their first turns in the snow. Across the way, Polaris Base Lodge houses ski and snowboard rental and

---

KIMBERLEY ALPINE RESORT

CENTRAL LINE
250-427-4881

CENTRAL RESERVATION LINE
800-258-SNOW (7669)

SNOW REPORT
250-427-7332

ANNUAL SNOWFALL
158 inches.

INFORMATION
www.skikimberley.com

SEASON
Early Dec—mid-April.

HOURS
Daily, 9 am—4 pm.
Night Skiing:
Nightly, 5 pm—9:30 pm.

repairs, ticket sales, guest services, condo units, lockers, ski school, an excellent daycare facility (250-427-4881) and the Stemwinder restaurant.

No matter how many improvements are made to the resort, the distance from major city centers ensures that the crowds are small and lift lines non-existent. Advanced skiers get their pick of great fall line trails that criss-cross through the forest. Or, they can head to the backside of the mountain for challenging glades and steeps. Beginners have their own area near the base and there are plenty of runs to please intermediate skiers on the front side of the mountain. There's also a half pipe and a terrain park for the snowboarding crew. Whichever chair you choose, all lifts have beginner trails that lead back to the base, so everyone can meet up for lunch.

The Bavarian town of Kimberley offers plenty of activities for families who want to take a breather from skiing. Kids love the waterpark, old-fashioned cinema and the bowling alley. Help cheer on the town's local junior hockey team, the Dynamiters, or shop along the pedestrian-only shopping mall, the Platzl. Be sure to examine the world's largest cuckoo clock and then stop in for a meal at the International Restaurant, where the chef's eccentric paraphernalia cover the walls. If you are staying a couple of weeks, sign the family up for a Skoki dog sledding course. More than just a ride, for $95 per person Eric and Aric will teach you how to master a team of huskies. You might even get a chance to head out on your own. If the family pet has also made the trip, schedule a ski-joring lesson. He'll soon be pulling your kids along on their skis. Other off-slope adventures include cross-country skiing, snowshoeing, skating and snowmobiling. Call 250-427-4881 for information and reservations.

Kimberley also offers an excellent assortment of nighttime activities. Every week mushers bring their dogs to the resort (kids can pet them), while a local guitarist plays old favorites around the campfire. If the kids want a night out, try the Kids Rule Outing. It's a two-hour program with children's activities such as arts and crafts, and movies are only $5 a child. Partake in a slew of family dinner options including a delightful evening at the Bauernhaus, located in Western Canada's oldest building.

👁 At a Glance

ADDRESS 301 North Star Boulevard, Kimberley, BC V1A 2Y5.

LOCATION Southeastern British Columbia.

TERRAIN MIX 1 mountains, 1,800 acres.

VERTICAL 2,465 feet (**PEAK** 6,500 feet. **BASE** 4,035 feet).

TRAILS 63 (20% Beginner, 45% Advanced, 35% Expert).

LIFTS 6 (1 high-speed quad, 2 triples, 2 doubles, 1 T-bar).

DAILY LIFT TICKET RATES (CDN) Adults $45, seniors (over 64), youths (13 to 17) and college students with ID $37, children (6 to 12) $15, under 6 free.

NIGHT SKIING TICKET RATES (CDN) Adults, seniors (over 64), youths (13 to 17) and college students with ID $15, children (6 to 12) $10, under 6 free.

SNOWMAKING None.

NIGHT SKIING Maverick T-bar services one of the longest lit runs in North America.

ACTIVITIES Snowshoeing, Nordic skiing, dog sledding, snowmobiling, Mountain Recreation Club (tennis, racquetball, squash, volleyball and fitness), ice-skating, heli-taxi service to Fernie Alpine Resort, waterpark, bowling, movie theater, Kids Rule!, campfires and sleigh rides.

BABYSITTERS Marriott Hotel (877-228-1948).

DAYCARE Kimberley Alpine Resort Daycare, daily, 8:30 am—4:30 pm (250-427-4881 ext. 251).

CHILDREN'S LESSONS AND CAMPS Discover Skiing and Discover Snowboarding, Kimberley Kruisers, Ski Scamps.

HOSPITAL Kimberley and District Hospital (250-427-2215).

SPECIAL DEALS Snow Guarantee, Louise Plus Card (discount card for anyone over 13). Fernie and Kimberly tickets are transferable.

SPECIAL PROGRAMS Adaptive sports for disabled skiers, Ladies' Day, Learn to Ski the Hard Stuff Program, Shape Ski Clinics.

GOOD MEETING PLACES Coffee Kiosk at Polaris (lower base), Day Lodge Cafeteria (upper base), Kootenay Haus (mid-mountain).

DISTANCES IN MILES Calgary, AB 253; Cranbrook Airport, BC 15; Edmonton, AB 400; Spokane, WA 209; Vancouver, BC 540.

OKANAGAN

Big White

This snow-packed region at the edge of the Monashee Mountains is a world-class ski destination. Located an hour east of Kelowna airport, Big White offers families the total package; hospitality, snow, sunshine, scenery, varied terrain and a host of après-ski activities.

Step off the plane, ride the shuttle from the airport to the resort's mid-mountain base and spend your time in Big White's village. It is easy to get around and there is no need for a rental car. At the Village Center, grab a snack at the bakery, then head upstairs for rentals, lift tickets or registration for ski school. If required, storage for your bags is available.

Your kids will love hopping aboard the gondola for a five-minute trip down to Happy Valley. Here, you'll find Big White's award-winning daycare (250-765-3101), plus an ice-skating rink, tubing area, a snowmobile circuit (with mini snowmobiles for kids) as well as beginner slopes serviced by magic carpets and surface tows. Dog sledding and the resort's Nordic trails are just a snowball's throw away.

Up top, Big White's slopes are every intermediate skier's dream. Accredited with the best grooming in western Canada by *Ski Canada*, the mountain offers skiers many blue runs that traverse through the forest. For experts, the recently expanded Westridge area offers a variety of advanced slopes. Got snowboard junkies in your family? Let them play on the resort's three half pipe terrain parks.

Family off-slope entertainment abounds at Big White. Check out the Activity Center in Big White Village Center and plan

BIG WHITE SKI RESORT

CENTRAL LINE
  800-663-2772
  or 250-765-3101

CENTRAL RESERVATION LINE
  800-663-2772

SNOW REPORT
  250-765-SNOW (7669)

ANNUAL SNOWFALL
  294 inches.

INFORMATION
  www.bigwhite.com

SEASON
  Late Nov—late April.

HOURS
  Daily, 8:45 am—3:30 pm.
  Tue—Sat, 5 pm—8 pm.

your evening. There's something for everyone. Play bingo, attend a Carnival night, see a movie or dine by torchlight. Need to relax? Stroll around the village, greet fellow skiers and warm up at one of the nightly bonfires.

Big White's lodging facilities offer excellent value and include three on-slope hotels, 21 condo buildings, 150 chalets and two youth hostels. Call the central reservation number for details (800-663-2772). Don't be surprised if your crew pleads to stay longer. With the range of activities, amenities and friendly services offered, be prepared to schedule a return visit.

◉ At a Glance

ADDRESS Box 2039, Station R, Kelowna, BC V1X 4K5.
LOCATION South central British Columbia.
TERRAIN MIX 1 mountains, 2,565 acres.
VERTICAL 2,646 feet (**PEAK** 7,606 feet. **BASE** 4,950 feet).
TRAILS 112 (18% Beginner, 30% Advanced, 26% More Difficult, 26% Expert).
LIFTS 13 (an 8-passenger gondola, 4 high-speed quads, 1 quad, 1 triple, 1 double, 1 surface, 1 magic carpet).
DAILY LIFT TICKET RATES (CDN) Adults $50, youths (13 to 18) $42, seniors (65 to 69) $35, children (6 to 12) $26, over 69 and under 6 free.
NIGHT LIFT TICKET RATES (CDN) Adults $17, youths (13 to 18) $17, seniors (65 to 69) $14, children (6 to 12) $14, over 69 and under 6 free.
SNOWMAKING None.
NIGHT SKIING 3 lifts, 38 acres, 1,624 vertical feet.
ACTIVITIES Tubing, snowmobiling, heli-skiing, ice-skating, sleigh rides, snowshoeing, dog sledding, spa, Nordic skiing, Kids after Dark, carnivals, fireworks, torchlight parades, campfires, Ladies day.
BABYSITTERS Kids Center (250-765-3101).
DAYCARE Kids Center, daily, 8:30 am—4 pm, 18 months to 6 years, (250-765-3101).
CHILDREN'S LESSONS AND CAMPS Ski & Snowboard School (250-765-3101 ext. 283).
HOSPITAL Whitefoot Medical, daily, 3 pm—6 pm (250-765-0544). Kelowna General Hospital (250-862-4000).
SPECIAL DEALS Free night skiing with purchase of multi-day lift ticket, 55+ program.
GOOD MEETING PLACES Happy Valley Lodge (beginner area) and Village Day Lodge.
DISTANCES IN MILES Calgary, AB 407; Kelowna, BC 34; Seattle, WA 345; Spokane, WA 283; Vancouver, BC 273.

Silver Star

Recently ranked in *Ski Canada* as the best skiing value in North America, Silver Star has long been one of Canada's premier family resorts. And for good reason. It boasts an excellent pedestrian village, a gamut of off-slope activities for kids of all ages, delicious dining options and superb ski conditions without losing the friendly feeling of a local's hill.

Silver Star is located one hour from Kelowna's International Airport and 20 minutes from the bustling town of Vernon. When you arrive, park your vehicle and let one of the resort's ambassadors help you get settled. Within a minute's walk, you can purchase lift tickets, ski rentals and sign up for lessons. On your way to the slope, drop the kids off at the new, spacious Kids' Center. Here, teens have their own Too Cool for School club. There's also a daycare center (250-558-6028) and lessons available for kids wanting to learn to ski or snowboard.

Once everyone's skis are strapped on, beginners should head to the Silver Queen chair, which is a slow-speed, low-to-the-ground lift separate from the rest of the resort. Intermediates have their choice of silky groomed trails, while advanced skiers can test their skills at the mountain's back bowls. When your brood feels peckish, head to Paradise Camp, a top-of-the-mountain funky eatery. Local chefs cook up some unusual dishes, such as buffalo burgers and exotic stews. Have cross-country skiers in your family? No problem. Several of the resort's 60 miles of Nordic ski trails run past Paradise Camp as well. Or dine at the Bugaboo's Bakery Café, situated in the resort's village at the base.

Want a break from carving those edges? Check out the activity center, open day and night. It offers fun activities such as tubing, ice-skating and snowmobiling (with mini-machines for kids). You can try night skiing on the slopes or on the three-mile track-set Nordic course. Visit the National High Altitude Training

---

SILVER STAR MOUNTAIN RESORT

CENTRAL LINE
800-663-4431
or 250-542-0224

CENTRAL RESERVATION LINE
877-663-4431

SNOW REPORT
250-542-1745

ANNUAL SNOWFALL
276 inches.

INFORMATION
www.skisilverstar.com

SEASON
Late Oct—mid-April.

HOURS
Daily, 8:30 am—3:30 pm (until 4:30 pm in the spring). Tue—Sat, 3:30 pm—9 pm.

Center and try the indoor rock-climbing wall, go for a swim or take an aerobics class. Twice a week, Silver Star offers a kids' program in the evenings where they can watch movies, go swimming or enjoy a kid-friendly supper. And if you're still searching for things to do, hop in the car and drive to Vernon to watch one of the best major-junior hockey teams in the country.

Due to Silver Star's intimate size, guests should book in advance. All beds are reserved through the central reservation number (800-663-4431), which means that with one phone call you can have your pick of accommodation, from a dorm room in a youth hostel to a luxurious five-bedroom Victorian home. No matter where your family chooses to stay, all accommodations are ski-in, ski-out. Silver Star plans to spend $150 million in improvements over the next few years, so the number of visitors to this fabulous resort is likely to skyrocket. Future guests can expect an expanded village, a new daycare center, more shopping and dining options and 500 acres of new, mostly intermediate terrain. Despite these changes, Silver Star will always remain a local's hill at heart. That's why the resort claims one of the highest repeat visitor ratios of any resort in North America.

☀ At a Glance

ADDRESS   Box 3002, Silver Star Mountain, BC V1B 3M1.
LOCATION   Southeastern British Columbia.
TERRAIN MIX   1 mountain, 3,065 acres.
VERTICAL   2,500 feet (**PEAK** 6,280 feet. **BASE** 3,780 feet).
TRAILS   107 (20% Beginner, 50% Advanced, 20% Expert, 10% Extreme).
LIFTS   10 (2 high-speed quads, 1 quad, 2 doubles, 2 surface, 2 magic carpet, 1 tube lift).
DAILY LIFT TICKET RATES (CDN)   Adults $45, youths (13 to 18) $23, seniors (over 70) $17, children (6 to 12) $15, under 6 free.
NIGHT SKIING TICKET RATES (CDN)   Adults and youths (13 to 18) $10.50, seniors (over 70) $6, under 6 free.
SNOWMAKING   None.
NIGHT SKIING   3 lifts, 1,000 feet vertical, 800 acres.
ACTIVITIES   2.5-mile lit Nordic track, free entertainment, tubing, sleigh rides, family night, snowmobiling, mini-snowmobiling, dog sledding, indoor pool, rock climbing, fitness center.
BABYSITTERS   Contact Star Kids Center (250-558-6028).
DAYCARE   Star Kids Center, daily, 8 am—4 pm, lunch included (250-558-6028).
CHILDREN'S LESSONS AND CAMPS   Star Kids Center (250-558-6028).
HOSPITAL   Vernon Jubilee Hospital (250-545-2211).

SPECIAL PROGRAMS Adaptive programs and Family Adventure weeks.
GOOD MEETING PLACES Bugaboos Bakery Café (base), Paradise Camp (on mountain).
GETTING AROUND Happy Bus, every 20 minutes, free.
DISTANCES IN MILES Kelowna, BC 35; Vancouver, BC 250.

Sun Peaks

A local skier's haven since the 1960s, Sun Peaks was "discovered" by a Japanese ski giant, Nippon Cable in the early 90s. The resort owners have invested over $275 million and received a number of awards, including best kids' resort, après-ski activities, terrain variety, grooming, village design and the Canadian Ski Industry's "friendliest locals" award.

The improvements made the mountain more family-friendly. Nippon Cable added five lifts providing access to more moderate terrain. They also created the pedestrian village, based on a colorful Tyrolean town. It boasts several full-service restaurants, pizzerias, a clock tower, ski and clothing stores. With so many visitors in the past few seasons, the resort is pumping an additional $70 million into improvements. Visitors can expect Mount Morrissey, a third mountain face, to open in the next year or two, complete with two lifts and 17 runs. Sun Peaks is also building a 230-room Delta Hotel and Convention Center and finishing off their 18-hole golf course.

Powder hounds will want to stop at the Village Day Lodge before heading off to the slopes. Here you'll find Snow Sports School registration, ski and snowboard rentals, guest services, Masa's Bar and Grill and a small café. Once you've gathered your gear, drop the tots off at Childminding Daycare (250-578-5433) —off-hour babysitting services are also

SUN PEAKS

CENTRAL LINE
250-578-7222

CENTRAL RESERVATION LINE
800-807-3257

SNOW REPORT
250-578-7232

ANNUAL SNOWFALL
220 inches.

INFORMATION
www.sunpeaksresort.com

SEASON
Mid-Nov—mid-April.

HOURS
Daily, 8:30 am—4 pm.
Tue, Thu the Platter lift stays open until 8 pm.

available. This comfy facility has an assortment of kids' stuff, including a covered magic carpet right outside the door. Parents feel secure with complimentary pagers the daycare provides. Older children should make their way to the Magic Carpet and Platter lift, while advanced riders hop aboard the Sundance quad and cruise down the excellent intermediate terrain (there are discounted tickets available for these lifts).

The Sunburst detachable quad drops you off at the small lodge and the adjacent multi-denominational chapel (services on Sundays at 1 pm). The Cahilty run (an excellent learning slope) is just off Sunburst. The trail connects with 5 Mile run and leads to the resort's longest chairlift, Crystal. This classic triple offers incredible vistas plus the mountain's greatest vertical drop at 2,891 feet. Experts can peek at the 360-degree panorama of British Columbia's interior before plunging into one of the back bowls or the black diamond Headwalls. For extreme skiers, traverse from Crystal chair or West Bowl T-bar to Executioner, Sun Peak's milestone double black diamond. Not a pro but want to catch the views? The whole family can ski down the resort's top-to-bottom green run that starts at Crystal chair.

When it's time to eat, grab a bite at Sunburst lodge or ski down to the numerous restaurants in the village. Bentos Day Lodge, a family favorite, is a cafeteria-style restaurant named after the Japanese box lunch. It has ample storage space for your coolers and lockers for your valuables. If you want something hot, there are two microwaves and a full-service cafeteria available.

For après-ski activity, head to Masa's Bar and Grill in the Village Day Lodge. Families will want to check out their Tuesday evening casino night. It's free to join and prizes are plentiful. As a bonus, kids' movies play on the large screen television during the festivities. If you're looking for some inexpensive fun, the Sports Center has two skating rinks, an outdoor pool, hot tub and weight room. Kids under six are free and everyone else pays a $6 entrance fee.

For down home comfort and charm, plan to stay at Nancy Greene's Cahilty Lodge (250-578-7454). It offers a variety of room choices, with options for kitchenettes and fireplaces. If you're there on Tuesday, you'll get to meet Nancy Greene, Canada's woman athlete of the century. On the slopes, you can almost always find her at 1:30 pm at the Sunburst quad. She might even give you a ski tip or two.

👁 At a Glance

ADDRESS 1280 Alpine Rd., Sun Peaks, BC V0E 1Z1.

LOCATION South central British Columbia.

TERRAIN MIX 2 mountains, 2,418 acres.

VERTICAL 2,891 feet (**PEAK** 6,824 feet. **BASE** 3,933 feet).

TRAILS 80 trails and 8 gladed areas (24% Beginner, 54% Advanced, 22% Expert).

LIFTS 8 (2 high-speed quads, 1 quad, 1 triple, 2 platter lifts, 2 magic carpets).

DAILY LIFT TICKETS RATES (CDN) Adults $48, youths (13 to 18) $41, seniors (over 64) $32, children (6 to 12) $27, under 6 free.

SNOWMAKING 3%.

NIGHT SKIING Tue and Thu the Platter lift stays open until 8 pm.

ACTIVITIES Torchlight dinners at the Sunburst lodge (mid-mountain), activity nights for kids, casino nights, film premiers, Nordic skiing, snowshoeing, snowmobiling, ice-skating, dog sledding.

BABYSITTERS Guest Services (250-578-5484).

DAYCARE Childminding Daycare (250-578-5433).

CHILDREN'S LESSONS AND CAMPS Sun Peaks Snow Sports School (250-578-5484).

HOSPITAL Doctor on premises 24 hours (250-578-5484). Royal Inland (250-374-5111).

SPECIAL DEALS Discover Sun Peaks Program (early-, mid- and late-season lift and lodging packages).

SPECIAL PROGRAMS Ski with Nancy Greene, First Tracks.

GOOD MEETING PLACES Snow Sports Ski School (in between Sunburst and Sundance chair).

DISTANCES IN MILES Calgary, AB 384; Kelowna, BC 101; Seattle, WA 288; Spokane, WA 354; Vancouver, BC 221.

WEST COAST

Whistler-Blackcomb

With over two million visitors annually, Canada's twin peaked mega-resort is drawing big crowds from around the globe. The reason? Whistler-Blackcomb serves up world-class on- and off-slope activities and amenities for a fraction of the price of its southern neighbors.

There are oodles of things for small snow hounds to do at Whistler-Blackcomb. With locations at each of the three bases (Whistler, Blackcomb and Creekside), Whistler Kids provides daycare services for those under three years of age. It also offers ski and snowboard lessons with over 500 instructors fluent in numerous languages. Their strict skier-to-instructor ratio guarantees your child personalized attention, but it also means classes fill up quickly, so it's a good idea to pre-register by calling (604-938-7310 or 800-766-0449). All Whistler Kids programs are parent-free, so adults can enjoy a hassle-free day while kids feel independent. Youngsters generally learn the ropes in the kids' terrain park, advancing to the trails when their skills improve. Each Whistler Kids location has arts and crafts supplies and nap rooms for tykes who need a break. They all have ski rental and tuning areas, as well as a gear shop for last minute items.

Beginners heading out on their own should stick to the lower lifts and trails. Blackcomb's Magic chair, the mid-station of the Whistler gondola and the Olympic chair are good starting points. The higher up you go, the tougher the terrain. Experts

WHISTLER-BLACKCOMB

CENTRAL LINE
800-766-0449
or 604-932-3434

CENTRAL RESERVATION LINE
888-403-4727

SNOW REPORT
800-766-0449

ANNUAL SNOWFALL
360 inches.

INFORMATION
www.whistler-blackcomb.com

SEASON
Late Nov—mid-June
(June—mid-Aug, skiing on Horstman Glacier).

HOURS
Daily, 9 am—3:30 pm
(opens at 8:30 am on weekends).

often head to Blackcomb's 7th Heaven or Whistler's Peak lift. If you prefer to frequent cruisers, head to the blue runs off the gondola. Snowboarders can test out the half pipe and Nintendo 64™ terrain park before venturing up to the more challenging Blackcomb Park. No matter where you ski or board, you can always ride the gondola (and select chairs) down the mountain. It's an excellent way to avoid packed base runs at the end of the day.

If you are staying a week or two, Whistler-Blackcomb has myriad après-ski options for the entire family. Plan to visit Meadow Park Sports Center, just two miles north of the resort. For $12, the whole family can ice-skate, swim, hot tub and enjoy the sauna, or use the weight room daily between 8:30 am and 9 pm. If you'd rather hang out close to your hotel, visit the Whistler Valley Activity Center for a current rundown of the resort's activity options. From movie going to bowling, mini-golfing to in-line skating, there are fun things to do every night of the week. All children (ages 18 months to 14 years) are welcome to take part in the nightly après-ski program from 4 pm to 6 pm and the Kid's Night Out program from 6 pm to 9 pm. Or, sign them up for a five-day Adventure Ski Camp, which includes group ski lessons plus a special après-ski activity on Thursday night.

Hungry? The resort boasts over 80 restaurants with something for every palate and budget. There are plenty of shops to poke around while strolling through the village, with many hotels just a stone's throw from the mountain. The four-star Westin (604-905-5000) offers family-oriented vacation packages, complete with a check-in bag of goodies (including hats, coloring books and special kid cups) and pre-recorded bedtime stories your kids can listen to on the telephone. For a less expensive option slightly off the beaten track, try Lost Lake Lodge, offering spacious condo units with fireplaces and washer/dryer facilities. Babysitting services are available through the Nanny Network (604-938-2823).

Whistler's free bus system, WAVE, makes it easy for the whole family to get around. Hop on the Perimeter Express Bus from the Vancouver airport (adults $53, kids $30) and you won't need a vehicle at all. So log on to www.tourismwhistler.com or call (800-WHISTLER) and book your next ski vacation at the Whistler-Blackcomb resort. Your kids will love the adventure-filled experience and you'll love the hospitality, security, and breathtaking views this Canadian resort serves up.

👁 At a Glance

ADDRESS 4545 Blackcomb Way, Whistler, BC V0N 1B4.

LOCATION 2 hours north of Vancouver.

TOTAL ACREAGE 7,071 acres.

VERTICAL Whistler Mountain: 5,020 feet (**PEAK** 7,160 feet. **BASE** 2,140 feet). Blackcomb Mountain: 5,280 feet (**PEAK** 7,494 feet. **BASE** 2,214 feet).

TRAILS Whistler Mountain: 100 (20% Beginner, 55% Intermediate, 25% Advanced). Blackcomb Mountain: 100 (15% Beginner, 55% Intermediate, 30% Advanced).

TOTAL LIFTS 33 (3 gondolas, 12 quads, 5 triples, 1 double, 4 T-bars, 7 tows, 1 magic carpet).

DAILY LIFT TICKETS RATES IN (CDN) Adults $61, seniors (over 64) and youths (13 to 18) $52, children (7 to 12) $31, under 7 free.

SNOWMAKING 555 acres.

NIGHT SKIING Wed and Sat one chair on Blackcomb open till 9 pm.

ACTIVITIES Nordic skiing, fishing, heli-skiing and boarding, paragliding, snowshoeing, dog sledding, horse-drawn sleigh rides, snowmobiling, swimming, ice-skating, library, museum, movie theatre, indoor tennis, Kid's Night Out, bowling, mini-golfing.

BABYSITTERS The Nanny Network (604-938-2823), Tiny Tots (604-938-4844).

DAYCARE Whistler Kids (604-932-3434).

CHILDREN'S CAMPS AND LESSONS Whistler Blackcomb Ski School (604-932-3434).

HOSPITAL Whistler Medical Center (604-932-4911).

SPECIAL DEALS Fresh Tracks, free mountain tours, avalanche awareness tours, welcome nights, week-long packages (800-284-9999).

SPECIAL PROGRAMS Ride Tribe, Ski Esprit, Women's only, Whistler Kids, Extremely Canadian.

GOOD MEETING PLACES Message boards at the bottom of lifts, top of lifts, Chic Pea, Horstman hut, Crystal hut.

GETTING AROUND WAVE in-resort bus shuttle, daily, free.

DISTANCE IN MILES Portland, OR 377; Seattle, WA 210; Vancouver, BC 100.

CHAPTER TWO

Northern Rockies and Utah

Montana, Wyoming, Idaho and Utah-area ski resorts compete for the huge market of diehard locals and destination skiers. With many families traveling to ski and board here, great savings are easy to come by. Families can also expect excellent discounts during the 2001-2002 Olympic season.

One of the best things about carving up slopes in the northern Rockies is that there's plenty of space for everyone. Without hub airports such as Denver, visitor numbers tend to be lower and so those who do make the trek enjoy few lift lines and fresh snow all season. Montana's Big Sky serves up huge terrain, incredible services, excellent family programming and one of the highest verticals in the United States. Jackson and Grand Targhee offer spectacular views of the Grand Tetons, with all the amenities and charm of the town of Jackson and side trips to Yellowstone National Park. Sun Valley, a North American classic, offers a kids-ski-free program, plus a beginners-only mountain.

Most of Utah's most renowned resorts are within a 45-minute drive from Salt Lake. Stick to the west side of the Wasatch Range (Alta, Brighton, Snowbird, Solitude) if you're into powder. Deer Valley, on the east-facing slopes, is a first-class luxury getaway spot. Families vacationing in the scenic south or visiting Las Vegas should head to Brian Head for its warm hospitality, boarding and snow tubing options.

Keep in mind that most Utah's resorts have peaks above 9,000 feet. If you're not used to heights, take it easy at first. Get acclimatized in nearby Park City or Salt Lake City before trekking out to the resort of your choice.

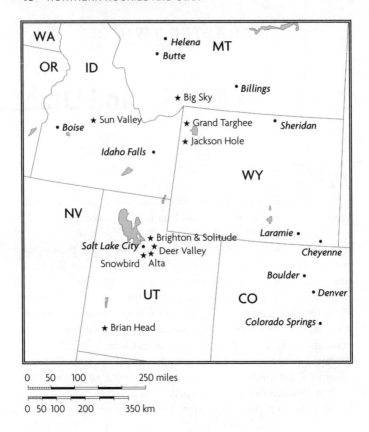

0   50   100   250 miles

0 50 100   200   350 km

Northern Rockies and Utah

Northern Rockies
- ★ Big Sky
- ★ Grand Targhee
- ★ Jackson Hole
- ★ Sun Valley

Utah
- ★ Alta
- ★ Brian Head
- ★ Brighton & Solitude
- ★ Deer Valley
- ★ Snowbird

NORTHERN ROCKIES

Big Sky

T here's something about Montana that makes you think of wide-open spaces and beautiful scenery. Luckily, there's no shortage of either at the state's most popular ski resort. Located only 45 miles from Bozeman, Big Sky is one destination your family won't want to miss. From Lone Mountain's majestic snow peak to the short lift lines to its proximity to Yellowstone National Park, Big Sky offers activities for the whole family and excellent prices to boot.

BIG SKY RESORT
CENTRAL LINE 406-995-5000
CENTRAL RESERVATION LINE 800-548-4486
SNOW REPORT 406-995-5900
ANNUAL SNOWFALL 400 inches.
INFORMATION www.bigskyresort.com
SEASON Nov—April.
HOURS Daily, 9 am—4 pm.

In recent years, renovations including a 15-person tram, four-star Summit Hotel and 100-person hot tub have catapulted Big Sky into the skiing big leagues. But families still find great deals (kids under 11 stay and ski for free), few lineups and all the amenities—restaurants, ski rentals, equipment and grocery stores. In addition, the resort is planning to open a larger pedestrian walk, with additional shops and facilities in the coming years.

When you get to Big Sky, head to the Snowcrest Day Lodge across from the Summit Hotel, where the Ski and Snowboard School (406-995-5743) and Handprints Daycare (406-995-3332) are located. Kids have ample space and toys to keep them occupied and happy. If they start to fuss, there are two rooms available for napping. State law requires that daycare visitors provide immunization records for every child. If anyone in your brood is taking lessons, they might get the chance to practice their German or Italian—many of the resort's ski instructors are part of an international exchange.

Big Sky's lift capacity sits at 20,000 per hour, but rarely does it see more than 5,000 visitors a day, making this mountain one of the ski industry's best kept secrets. For those just starting out, there's a 220-foot magic carpet serviced slope to practice snow-plowing. Beginners and skiers getting back into the swing of things can check out the spacious Mr. K. and White-Wing greens. Alongside these trails, intermediates will find smooth runs and slightly steeper pitches. Try out Calamity Jane and Lobo before heading over to the advanced Andesite. For a bigger challenge, experts can strut their stuff on the trails off Lone Peak Tram. Test your mettle down Big Couloir or any of the Gullies, or trek over to Challenger chair for your choice of seven black diamond runs.

Whatever lift your family chooses, there's always a way down to the heart of the pedestrian village, where lunches range from French fries to filet mignons. Big Sky menus cover all things Western. For evening entertainment try Huntley Lodge, where arts and crafts, games and dog rescue programs begin at 5 pm. For the more active, the skating rink is open until 11 pm ($4 for skate rentals). Cinema buffs should head over to Yellowstone Conference Center amphitheater which features free nightly ski and family movies. If you want some off-slope adventures, try one of these many options. Take a relaxing break and ride the Yellowstone National Park snow coach, or spend a day in the spa. Need more excitement? Go snowmobiling or winter fly fishing on the Gallatin—segments of Robert Redford's *A River Runs Through It* were shot on this river.

Guests have two main choices for accommodations. Families can stay slope-side in one of the hotels (The Summit, Huntley Lodge, Arrowhead Chalets, Beaverhead, Shoshone, Cedar Creek or Snow Crest lodges), or grab the shuttle and overnight in the cheaper Meadow Village, just three miles south. Call central reservations at 800-538-4486.

Although Big Sky is a bit farther afield than resorts in Utah or Colorado, you'll make up the extra travel time by never having to wait in lift lines. With improved air service—United Airlines now offers daily service between Denver and Bozeman —it's easy to get to Big Sky.

👁 At a Glance

ADDRESS P.O. Box 160001, Big Sky, MT 59716.
LOCATION Southwestern Montana.
TERRAIN MIX 3 mountains, 3,600 acres.
VERTICAL 4,366 feet (**PEAK** 11,166 feet. **BASE** 6,800 feet).
TRAILS 122 (10% Beginner, 47% Advanced, 43% Expert).
LIFTS 18 (a 15-person tram, a 4-person gondola, 3 high-speed quads,
 1 quad, 4 triples, 4 doubles, 3 surface, 1 magic carpet).
DAILY LIFT TICKET RATES (US) Adults $54, seniors $27, students with ID and
 youths (11 to 17) $42, under 11 free.
SNOWMAKING 10%.
NIGHT SKIING None.
ACTIVITIES Sleigh ride dinners, moonlight Snowcat dinners, movies,
 children's activity nights, aerobics, snowshoeing, snowmobiling, Nordic
 skiing, fly fishing, dog sledding, Yellowstone National Park tours,
 helicopter tours, horseback riding, massage and spa, Snowcat skiing.
BABYSITTERS 406-995-3332 or 406-995-5806.
DAYCARE Handprints Daycare, 6 months to 10 years, reservations and
 immunizations required (406-995-3332).
CHILDREN'S LESSONS AND CAMPS International Ski and Snowboard School,
 Teen Mountain Experience (406-995-5743).
HOSPITAL Bozeman Deaconess Hospital (406-585-5000).
SPECIAL DEALS Frequency Card Program (reduced rates).
SPECIAL PROGRAMS Telemark lessons, avalanche dog presentations, free
 mountain tours, private mountain guides for the tram and Challenger
 chair.
GOOD MEETING PLACES M.R. Hummers in the Mountain Mall (base), The
 Dugout (on-slope).
GETTING AROUND Snow Express, daily, 7 am to 11 pm, free.
DISTANCES IN MILES Bozeman, MT 38; Boise, ID 704; Gallatin Airport, MT
 50; Helena, MT 131; Seattle, WA 710; West Yellowstone, WY 40.

Grand Targhee

Grand Targhee is the ultimate deep-snow mountain. Nestled on the western face of the Grand Tetons, the resort sits at the confluence of the southwestern storm track, collecting huge amounts of snow each year. In fact, the powder is so tremendous, it's guaranteed! If you don't like the conditions, return your ticket within the first hour and get a full refund.

Families love Targhee for its expansive intermediate terrain, lack of crowds and authentic western feel. At 8,000 feet, the resort offers spectacular views of the mountain, a simple pedestrian village and a single base, making it easy for kids to get around. If you're planning on staying overnight, pick up some groceries in town before driving up to Targhee—keep in mind that local stores are closed on Sundays. If you're riding the airport shuttle (approximately $70 per person round-trip from either Jackson or Idaho Falls), it stops in town for supplies.

Fewer amenities mean the resort is primarily a skiers' mountain. Neophytes love the wide-open beginner area, serviced by a magic carpet and slow-speed quad. Intermediates test their mettle on the slopes covered with powder. Skiers looking for a little more challenge can sign up for Targhee's famous Cat skiing program and gain access to fresh snow on neighboring peaks. Or take to the backcountry for some excellent carving and spectacular views of the Tetons. Contact Rich Rinaldi's Yöstmark Tours for details (208-354-2828). If you're new to skiing powder, the Snow Sports School offers instruction in boarding, skiing and telemarking. Have teens in your crew? They'll definitely want to join the Powder Scouts and enjoy the adult-free facility at the base. Extreme skiers should plan to attend the annual X-Team clinic offered in December.

GRAND TARGHEE

CENTRAL LINE
800-TARGHEE (827-4433)
or 307-353-2300

CENTRAL RESERVATION LINE
800-TARGHEE (827-4433)

SKI REPORT
800-TARGHEE (827-4433)

ANNUAL SNOWFALL
504 inches.

INFORMATION
www.grandtarghee.com

SEASON
Mid-Nov—mid-April.

HOURS
Daily, 9:30 am—4 pm.

Need a break from skiing? For $15 you can rent one of SnowPlay Outfitters' ski-bikes or ski-scooters for your kids. Partake in the mellow après-ski activities the resort provides nightly. If you stay at any of the resort's condos, your kids will sleep in bunk beds. There are also accommodation specials before Christmas. Call 800-827-4433 for details.

Look for changes to be implemented in the next few years. Long-time Targhee skier George Gillett took over the resort's operation in 2000 and plans to add a high-speed quad to access 500 acres on Targhee's second mountain, called Peaked. Overnight guests will soon experience improved accommodation and convention facilities. Because of Targhee's isolated locale, large-scale improvements won't change the sprawling, uncrowded, friendly atmosphere the resort is famous for—and who can resist the annual snowfall of over 500 inches?

👁 At a Glance

ADDRESS   Ski Hill Road, Alta, WY 83422.

LOCATION   1 hour northwest of Jackson.

TERRAIN MIX   2 mountains, 3,000 acres.

VERTICAL   Fred's Mountain: 2,200 feet (**PEAK** 10,200 feet. **BASE** 8,000 feet). Peaked Mountain: 2,822 feet (**PEAK** 10,230 feet. **BASE** 7,408 feet).

TRAILS   103 (10% Beginner, 70% Advanced, 20% Expert).

LIFTS   4 (1 high-speed quad, 1 quad, 1 double, 1 magic carpet).

DAILY LIFT TICKET RATES (US)   Adults $44, seniors (over 61) $24, children (6 to 14) $27, under 6 free.

SNOWMAKING   None.

NIGHT SKIING   None.

ACTIVITIES   Horse-drawn sleigh dinners, tubing, movies, casino nights, Forest Service slide shows, Nordic skiing, snowshoe tours, dog sledding, outdoor heated pool, hot tub, spa, fitness center, snowmobiling in Yellowstone and Grand Teton National Parks, ice-skating.

BABYSITTERS   800-827-4433 ext. 1362.

DAYCARE   Kids Club, 2 months to 5 years (800-827-4433 ext. 1362).

CHILDREN'S LESSONS AND CAMPS   Snowsports School (800-827-4433 ext. 1352).

HOSPITAL   Teton Valley Hospital (208-354-2383).

SPECIAL DEALS   Teewinot Lodge vacations (book before Oct 1), snow guarantee, children (under 14) ski and stay for free, free Snowcat skiing for pre-Christmas bookings.

SPECIAL PROGRAMS   Cat skiing, Yöstmark backcountry tours, X-Team advanced ski clinic, NASTC Powder Clinic, mountain guide program.

GOOD MEETING PLACES   Village clock tower, Rendezvous Lodge.

DISTANCES IN MILES   Idaho Falls, ID 87; Jackson, WY 44; Salt Lake City, UT 297.

Jackson Hole

Long known as one of the most challenging mountains on the continent, this American classic comes complete with fantastic terrain, authentic Western charm and a blizzard of après-ski and winter activities. Add on its proximity to Grand Teton and Yellowstone National Parks, and the variety of services offered in the town of Jackson, and you've got a first-rate family vacation destination.

In its recent multi-million dollar expansion, Jackson Hole Mountain Resort has created one of the finest children's facilities in the west. Located across from Bridger Center, Kid's Ranch at Cody House has an excellent daycare facility (307-739-2691). Here you'll find the ski school, rental shop, technicians, overnight ski storage, kitchen and dining facilities, and a kid's specialty retail store. Fort Wyoming, a sports playground with colorful Western-style ski-through characters and teepees for kids to visit, is just outside the door.

Older children have a number of ski school options. The resort offers very popular ski and snowboard Adrenaline Camps led by Olympian and World Cup racers. Also popular are the Team Extreme camps for teens and specialized Freestyle and Steep & Deep camps for advanced skiers. All lessons include the interactive Ske-cology program, which combines ski and boarding lessons with environmental awareness. If you're an advanced skier and want to maximize your visit to Jackson, hire a backcountry guide and explore the mountain's huge off-piste terrain (800-450-0477).

> **JACKSON HOLE MOUNTAIN RESORT**
>
> **CENTRAL LINE**
> 800-443-8613
> or 307-733-2292
>
> **CENTRAL RESERVATION LINE**
> 888-333-7766
> or 307-733-2292
>
> **SNOW REPORT**
> 307-733-4005
>
> **ANNUAL SNOWFALL**
> 402 inches.
>
> **INFORMATION**
> www.jacksonhole.com
>
> **SEASON**
> Early Dec—early April.
>
> **HOURS**
> Daily, 9 am—4 pm.

For families who are skiing or snowboarding on their own, keep in mind the terrain is tougher than most resorts. All of the beginner runs are located at the Bridger Base and are accessed by either Teewinot quad or Eagle's Rest double. For more experienced skiers, ride the high-speed Apres Vous quad for good views and some excellent blue slopes. Advanced skiers can hit the bumps and glades off the Bridger Gondola. Experts should hop aboard the tram for some heart-stopping steeps including the classic Corbet's Couloir atop Rendezvous Peak. Beginners and intermediates can ride the lift up and down for a look at the quintessential Jackson experience without having to ski the descent.

Getting together for lunch with the family is easy. The on-slope Casper Restaurant is the mountain's largest dining area. However it is only accessed by intermediate and expert terrain.

Families with beginners can meet at Nick Wilson's Cowboy Café located in the tram building at the base. The small-sized restaurant tends to fill up quickly so eating early or late is your best chance for getting a table.

The Saddlehorn Nordic Center (307-739-2629) is the one-stop shop for snowshoe, cross-country ski rentals and dog sledding in the valley. With Yellowstone's world famous geysers just 45 minutes away, nobody should miss taking a tour of the National Park by snowmobile or snow coach. Shoppers should head straight for town—located just ten minutes from the resort, Jackson has all the specialty boutiques and restaurants you'd expect from a vibrant, world-class tourist destination.

If you still have energy to burn when the sun goes down, try ice-skating and shinny hockey on the municipal rink, or tubing and night skiing at Snow King, Jackson's local hill. If you'd rather be inside, spend $5 and catch a hockey game between Jackson and a visiting minor league team. Stop by the library for excellent evening programs and facilities for kids.

There are two locations for accommodation. Stay slope-side in Teton Village where evenings are decidedly quiet, or get a room in Jackson. Both places have a wide selection, from hostels to full-service hotels to luxury condos. It's cheaper to stay in town but you won't need a car in either place. For $2 a person, START (Southern Teton Area Rapid Transit) bus service is the easiest way to get between town and the resort. No matter where you choose to stay, the amenities, service and warm hospitality served up at Jackson Hole Mountain Resort will keep everyone in your family entertained and happy.

◉ At a Glance

ADDRESS P.O. Box 290/3395 McCollister Dr., Teton Village, WY 83025.
LOCATION 15 minutes north of Jackson.
TERRAIN MIX 2 mountains, 2,500 acres (3,000 acres in surrounding backcountry).
VERTICAL 4,139 feet (**PEAK** 10,450 feet. **BASE** 6,311 feet).
TRAILS 80 (10% Beginner, 40% Advanced, 50% Expert).
LIFTS 11 (a 63-person tram, an 8-person gondola, 2 high-speed quads, 4 quads, 1 triple, 1 double, 1 magic carpet).
DAILY LIFT TICKET RATES (US) Adults $56, seniors and children (6 to 14) $28, youths (15 to 21) $43, under 6 free.
SNOWMAKING 5%.

NIGHT SKIING   None.
ACTIVITIES   Dinner sleigh rides (307-739-2603), snowshoeing, cross-country skiing, dog sledding, telemarking, Yellowstone and Grand Teton National Parks tours, Vertical Foot Club membership (loyalty program that records vertical feet skied during your vacation), backcountry skiing (800-450-0477).
BABYSITTERS   307-739-2691.
DAYCARE   Kids Ranch, daily, 8:30 am—4 pm, 2 months to 5 years, reservations required (307-739-2691).
CHILDREN'S LESSONS AND CAMPS   Jackson Hole Ski and Snowboard School, Wild West Adrenaline Camp Series (800-450-0477 or 307-739-2663).
HOSPITAL   St. John's Hospital (307-733-3636).
SPECIAL DEALS   Visit www.jhresortlodging.com or call (800-443-8613).
GOOD MEETING PLACES   Bridger Center (gondola base), Nick Wilson's Cowboy Café (clock tower building at the tram base).
GETTING AROUND   START Bus, daily, 6:30 am—10:30 pm ($2).
DISTANCES IN MILES   Boise, ID 300; Cheyenne, WY 370; Helena, MT 300; Idaho Falls, ID 90; Jackson, WY 10; Salt Lake City, UT 250.

Sun Valley

Nestled between Idaho's semi-arid desert and the stately Smokey Mountain Range, Sun Valley is endowed with plenty of the best ingredients for a winter destination—warm, sunny days. Developed in 1936 as the nation's premier ski and summer resort by railway tycoon Averell Harriman, Sun Valley boasts a long history of skiing firsts, including the creation of the chairlift prototype and the first North American Winter Olympic Gold Medallist, Gretchen Fraser. The resort also owns the world's finest automated snowmaking equipment—the $20 million investment guarantees great skiing from November to April.

How does your family fit into all this? Easy. Only five hours from Salt Lake City, Sun Valley has always attracted Utah's large family market with their incredible deals. For example, kids under 16 ski for free from

SUN VALLEY

CENTRAL LINE
208-622-4111

CENTRAL RESERVATION LINE
800-634-3347
or 208-726-3423

SNOW REPORT
800-635-4150

ANNUAL SNOWFALL
200 inches.

INFORMATION
www.sunvalley.com

SEASON
Mid-Nov—late April.

HOURS
Daily, 9 am—4 pm.

Thanksgiving to mid-December, most of January and from mid-March to the end of the season (one child per parent). And at many of the hotels in Sun Valley, kids stay free. If you're flying, check out Southwest Vacations and ask about the "under 14 fly free" package (www.swavacations.com or 800-435-9792).

The resort consists of two mountains. The beginner-only Dollar Mountain is accessed from Sun Valley. Bald Mountain, a 3,400 foot vertical massif is located in Ketchum, a mile from the village. KART, the local free shuttle that operates daily from 8 am until midnight, makes it easy to get around. If you're driving, the best parking facilities are at River Run. Have beginners with you? The Sun Valley Ski School busses them to and from the parking lot and Dollar Mountain, so you won't have to stop twice.

Dollar Mountain's 13 runs are serviced by a magic carpet, handle tow and four chairlifts (none of the chairlifts have security bars). If you're looking for some beginner slopes at Bald Mountain, try Upper and Lower College runs. They have excellent pitch. Otherwise, Bald Mountain serves up plenty of advanced and expert terrain. Wherever you choose to carve those edges, you won't be waiting in line. The resort averages 3,000 skiers a day with the lift capacity at 28,180 per hour.

Looking for a little culture? Sun Valley was recently ranked 18th in *The 100 Best Small Art Towns in America*. There's local theater, innumerable galleries, cultural centers and the town library with reading nights and other programs for families. Call the Chamber of Commerce for details (800-634-3347).

Most guests stay at the famous Sun Valley Lodge (800-786-8259) because the amenities and service are world-class. There's a bowling alley, a top-notch spa, an indoor and outdoor skating rink, numerous restaurants, sleigh ride dinners to Trail Creek Cabin, an Opera House showing first run movies, two pools, hot tubs, saunas and the newly expanded Valley Massage Center. For families looking for more reasonably priced condos, Base Mountain Properties (800-521-2515 or 208-726-5601) has three-story rentals with full kitchens, fireplaces and yards. Call the Sun Valley Central Reservations for all other listings (800-634-3347).

👁 At a Glance

ADDRESS   P.O. Box 10, Sun Valley, ID 83353.

LOCATION   Central Idaho.

TERRAIN MIX   2 mountains, 2054 acres.

VERTICAL   Bald Mountain: 3,400 feet (**PEAK** 9,150 feet. **BASE** 5,570 feet).
Dollar Mountain: 628 feet (**PEAK** 6,638 feet. **BASE** 6,010 feet).

TRAILS   Bald Mountain: 78 (36% Beginner, 42% Advanced, 22% Expert).
Dollar Mountain: 13 (70% Beginner, 30% Advanced).

LIFTS   20 (7 high-speed quads, 5 triples, 5 doubles, 2 surface, 1 magic
carpet).

DAILY LIFT TICKETS RATES (US)   Bald Mountain: Adults $59, seniors (over 64)
$40, under 13 $33. Dollar Mountain: Adults $24, seniors (over 64) $16,
under 13 $17.

SNOWMAKING   33%.

NIGHT SKIING   None.

ACTIVITIES   Theater, ice-skating, swimming, galleries, movies, bowling, fine
dining, free showings of "Sun Valley Serenade" in the Opera House.

BABYSITTERS   208-622-2288 or 208-788-5080.

DAYCARE   Sun Valley Playschool, daily, 8:30 am—4:30 pm (208-622-2288).
Super Sitters (208-788-5080).

CHILDREN'S LESSONS AND CAMPS   Sun Valley Ski & Snowboard School, Tiny
Tracks (3 to 4), Dollar Mountain Clinics (4 to 12) (800-786-8259).

HOSPITAL   St. Luke's Medical Center (208-727-8800).

SPECIAL DEALS   Kids under 15 stay and ski free program during select weeks
(800-786-8259).

SPECIAL PROGRAMS   Women's clinics, Master's Race clinics, adaptive lessons.

GOOD MEETING PLACES   At the fireplaces of River Run Lodge, Seattle Ridge
Lodge and Warm Springs Lodge.

DISTANCE IN MILES   Boise, ID 173; Salt Lake City, UT 293.

UTAH

Alta

High in the glaciated Little Cottonwood Canyon, the snow hasn't just frozen the peaks—it has also frozen time. At the beginning of the last century, Alta was a booming mining town. By the 1930s, the natural resources were exhausted and the settlers left—all except George Watson. He had fallen in love with the area and decided to reinvent Alta as a skier's oasis. Watson deeded 1,800 acres to the Forestry Service (the mountain badly needed to be reforested) and engaged the support of Salt Lake businessmen to finance his dream. Within years, the mountain began to take shape as a skier's haven.

Naturally endowed with great terrain, Alta also boasts some of the best powder on the planet—each year it sees over 500 inches. Watson's ingenuity drew legendary skiers such as Al Engen, who wanted to ride the Alta lift (the third chair in North America). Engen pioneered early powder techniques and founded Alta's Ski School in 1948. But it is Alta's philosophy, built around protecting the skiing experience that has created a sense of timelessness about the mountain. Instead of following the standard method of development, the resort limits traffic by disallowing snowboarders, controlling the number of day passes sold and refusing bus charters. For families, this means safer skiing, better conditions and more time to enjoy the experience.

Upon arrival, families stop at the Alta Children's Center located at the Albion base. In this cozy facility, there's plenty to keep youngsters busy. Base area rope tows offer free skiing to beginners and are used for ski school lessons. The Albion and

ALTA SKI AREA

CENTRAL LINE
801-359-1078

CENTRAL RESERVATION LINE
888-782-9258

SNOW REPORT
801-359-1078

ANNUAL SNOWFALL
500 inches.

INFORMATION
www.alta.com

SEASON
Mid-Nov—mid-April.

HOURS
Daily, 9:15 am—4:30 pm.

Sunnyside chairs provide access to some of the best beginner-only terrain in the country, or ride the Sugarloaf detachable triple for a scenic descent on Crooked Mile. Alf Engen's Ski School is the perfect place to learn powder skiing. While you sharpen your skills, ski instructors at Alta share stories about what it's like to live in a remote community of only 400 people.

Families visiting Alta for the first time will want to experience Alta Lodge (800-707-ALTA). There's a complimentary kid's program, which includes après-ski activities such as games, arts and crafts, a special meal and an after dinner movie. Occasional talks and slide shows in the evenings are good for the whole family. Adults can lounge in the Sitzmark club or enjoy coffee in the lobby before the day begins. Be sure to reserve ahead because Alta Lodge has the highest return rate in the ski industry. Over 80 percent of its guests come back year after year. If you'd rather, stay locally at one of the many other accommodations or commute to Snowbird for the evening. Call ahead for information (800-453-3000).

Skiing at Alta is a step back in time. Keep in mind you can't snowboard, there are no high-speed lifts and no pedestrian village. People come here to enjoy the rustic, old-fashioned ski experience without the glitz and glam of modern resorts.

👁 At a Glance

ADDRESS P.O. Box 8007, Alta, UT 84092-8007.

LOCATION Northern Utah.

TERRAIN MIX 3 mountains, 2,200 acres.

VERTICAL 2,020 feet (**PEAK** 10,550 feet. **BASE** 8,530 feet).

TRAILS 40 (25% Beginner, 40% Advanced, 35% Expert).

LIFTS 13 (3 triples, 5 doubles, 5 surface lifts).

DAILY LIFT TICKETS RATES (US) Tickets issued based on lifts used. All lifts $35, beginner lifts only $25, seniors (over 80) ski free.

SNOWMAKING 50 acres.

NIGHT SKIING None.

ACTIVITIES None.

BABYSITTERS Contact individual lodges.

DAYCARE Alta Children's Center, daily, 8:30 am—5:30 pm, 3 months to 12 years (801-742-3042).

CHILDREN'S LESSONS AND CAMPS Alf Engen Ski School, Children Ski Adventures (801-359-1078 or 801-742-3333).

HOSPITAL Alta View Hospital (801-501-2231).

SPECIAL PROGRAMS Ske-cology programs, tour with a ranger, mountain hosts, "Diamond Challenge" for expert skiers.

GOOD MEETING PLACES   Alf's Restaurant, Alta Children's Center at Albion Base, Albion Grill.
GETTING AROUND   Canyon Transportation Van Service (800-225-1841) or Utah Transit Authority (801-287-4636).
DISTANCES IN MILES   Denver, CO 545; Salt Lake City, UT 25.

Brian Head

Brian Head's cozy alpine hideaway has become a favorite winter playground for Las Vegas residents. Tucked into the Grand Circle of National Parks and just three hours from the big city, this small-scale, family-owned resort serves up a peaceful ski experience with virtually no lift lines, plenty of family discounts and boundless hospitality.

Families with new skiers start off at Navajo Lodge. It's the hub for beginners and children's programs, including Kids Camp — ski and boarding lessons for those under 12. There's a rental shop downstairs and Brian Head's daycare for infants to six year olds, is on the premises (435-677-2047). Also at Navajo, families can enjoy tubing between 10 am and 4 pm weekdays and until 10 pm on weekends. The local medical clinic is located here too (435-677-2700).

While beginners stick to the runs outside Navajo, advanced skiers trek across the street to Giant Steps (free bus service between bases). Hop aboard the Snow Cat Peak Express (weather permitting) to access Brian Head peak's breathtaking views and heart-pounding steeps. Giant Steps is also home to an extensive terrain park for boarders.

Aside from skiing, boarding and tubing, Brian Head provides other activities including backcountry snowmobile tours, National Park sightseeing and an extensive network of Nordic and snowshoeing trails. A five-minute drive south of Brian Head

BRIAN HEAD RESORT

CENTRAL LINE
435-677-2035

CENTRAL RESERVATION LINE
800-27-BRIAN (27426)

SNOW REPORT
435-677-2035

ANNUAL SNOWFALL
425 inches.

INFORMATION
www.brianhead.com

SEASON
Early Nov — late April.

HOURS
Daily, 9:30 am — 4:30 pm (until 10 pm on weekends and holidays).

brings you to Cedar Breaks National Monument, a giant red-rock amphitheater full of pinnacles and buttresses that's over 2,500 feet deep and three miles across.

Guests can expect a full range of slope-side hotels and condos at Brian Head. The resort's full service Cedar Breaks Hotel (888-ATCEDAR) is a classic choice, along with many other possibilities. The free bus shuttle services all the local lodgings. For a great place to dine, try the family-favorites Bump and Grind deli or Pasta Luna.

👁 At a Glance

ADDRESS P.O. Box 19008, Brian Head, UT 84719.

LOCATION Southern Utah.

TERRAIN MIX 2 mountains, 500 acres.

VERTICAL 1,320 feet (**PEAK** 10,307 feet. **BASE** 8,087 feet).

TRAILS 53 (30% Beginner, 40% Intermediate, 30% Advanced).

LIFTS 9 (5 triples, 1 double, 3 surface).

DAILY LIFT TICKET RATES (US) Adults $38, seniors (over 64) and children (6 to 12) $25, under 6 free. Rates increase by $2 during certain holidays.

NIGHT LIFT TICKET RATES (US) Flat rate $8.

SNOWMAKING 35%.

NIGHT SKIING Pioneer lift (beginner terrain).

ACTIVITIES Burn Rubber snow tubing park, Nordic skiing, snowshoeing, snowmobiling, National Park tours, spa, snow-bike rentals.

BABYSITTERS Call the concierge at the Cedar Breaks Lodge (435-677-3000).

DAYCARE Kids Camp, daily, 9 am—4:45 pm, infants to 12 years, reservations required (435-677-2047).

CHILDREN'S LESSONS AND CAMPS Kids Camp (435-677-2047).

HOSPITAL Valley View Medical Hospital (435-586-6587).

SPECIAL DEALS Snow Fun 101 (2 lessons with equipment and a free season pass).

GOOD MEETING PLACES Giant Steps Lodge (base), Navajo Lodge (base).

GETTING AROUND Free local bus shuttle.

DISTANCES IN MILES Las Vegas, NV 200; Phoenix, AZ 500; Salt Lake City, UT 253.

Brighton & Solitude

Although Brighton and Solitude may not offer the same vertical as their southern neighbors, they both average 500 inches of Utah powder per year. Situated on the western slope of the Wasatch range in Big Cottonwood Canyon, these two resorts serve up plenty of family fun and are an excellent two-in-one package destination.

About 28 miles from Salt Lake City, Solitude prides itself on being the quietest resort in the state. Families are drawn by minimal lineups, an abundance of beginner and intermediate terrain and its laid-back attitude, which makes learning to ski powder a pleasant experience. Brighton is just two miles down the road and has become Utah's snowboarding haven. Not surprisingly, it is also a prime teen hangout.

While neither resort offers daycare, families ski here because both offer free lift passes to kids under 11 (two per paying adult). Furthermore, ski school is an affordable alternative to babysitters if parents want to ski alone. Both resorts offer half-day ski and ride lessons for $45.

When it's time to get together, hungry Brighton carvers can rendezvous at the cozy, warm Brighton Center. Solitude's old-style Moonbeam Center is the best place for families to eat, since it houses the ski school and its lifts access beginner terrain. More significantly, there's better parking than in the village lot.

Solitude has teamed up with Canadian real estate giant Intrawest to

BRIGHTON SKI RESORT

CENTRAL LINE
801-532-4731

CENTRAL RESERVATION LINE
800-873-5512

SNOW REPORT
801-532-4731

ANNUAL SNOWFALL
500 inches.

INFORMATION
www.skibrighton.com

SEASON
Early Nov—late April.

HOURS
Daily, 9 am to 4 pm.
(until 9 pm Mon—Sat
from Dec—early April).

SOLITUDE MOUNTAIN RESORT

CENTRAL LINE
801-534-1400

CENTRAL RESERVATION LINE
800-748-4754

SNOW REPORT
801-536-5777

ANNUAL SNOWFALL
500 inches.

INFORMATION
www.skisolitude.com

SEASON
Early Nov—late April.

HOURS
Daily, 9 am—4 pm.

develop an upscale ski village to complement its own charming Mountain Inn. The small pedestrian area offers various dining opportunities, from family-priced menus to fine cuisine. Down the road, the Brighton Lodge offers limited scope with only 20 rustic motel-style rooms. However, Brighton serves up an ever-popular night ski option, while at Solitude evening entertainment is limited to watching videos.

◉ At a Glance

BRIGHTON

ADDRESS Star Route, Brighton, UT 84121.

LOCATION Northern Utah.

TERRAIN MIX 4 mountain peaks, 850 acres.

VERTICAL 1,745 feet (**PEAK** 10,500 feet. **BASE** 8,755 feet).

TRAILS 66 (21% Beginner, 40% Advanced, 39% Expert).

LIFTS 8 (3 high-speed quads, 1 triple, 3 doubles, 1 surface).

DAILY LIFT TICKETS RATES (US) Adults $37, seniors (over 69) $10, children under 11 free.

SNOWMAKING 20%.

NIGHT SKIING 20 runs, over 200 acres.

ACTIVITIES Nordic skiing.

BABYSITTERS None.

DAYCARE None.

HOSPITAL Alta View Hospital (801-501-2231).

SPECIAL DEALS Intro and Works (offer a lesson, lift ticket and rentals), reduced price for Adult Learner lift ticket ($25).

SPECIAL PROGRAMS Discover! Tour with a Ranger to learn about the Wasatch forest, mountain host tours.

GOOD MEETING PLACES Molly Green's (base of Majestic), Brighton chalet (base of Millicent).

GETTING AROUND Free Shuttle to Nordic Center, UTA offers complete canyon transport (801-BUS-INFO).

DISTANCES IN MILES Denver, CO 545; Salt Lake City, UT 28.

SOLITUDE

ADDRESS 12,000 Big Cottonwood Canyon, Solitude, UT 84121.

LOCATION Northern Utah.

TERRAIN MIX 1 mountain, 1,200 acres.

VERTICAL 2,047 feet (**PEAK** 10,035 feet. **BASE** 7,988 feet).

TRAILS 63 (20% Beginner, 50% Advanced, 30% Expert).

LIFTS 7 (1 high-speed quad, 2 triples, 4 doubles).

DAILY LIFT TICKET RATES (US) Adults $39, seniors (60 to 69) $29, over 69 and under 11 free.

SNOWMAKING 9%.

NIGHT SKIING None.

ACTIVITIES   Nordic skiing.
BABYSITTERS   801-534-1400.
DAYCARE   None.
CHILDREN'S LESSONS AND CAMPS   Ski School (801-536-5730).
HOSPITAL   Alta View Hospital (801-501-2231).
SPECIAL DEALS   Call for details (800 748-4SKI).
SPECIAL PROGRAMS   None.
GOOD MEETING PLACES   Last Chance Mining Camp (base).
GETTING AROUND   Free Shuttle to Nordic Center, UTA offers complete canyon transport (801-BUS-INFO).
DISTANCES IN MILES   Denver, CO 545; Salt Lake City, UT 28.

Deer Valley

Consistently rated number one by readers of *Ski Magazine* in the areas of dining, guest services and mountain grooming, it's little wonder families flock to Deer Valley. While this skier's paradise is more expensive than some other resorts, it is committed to providing top-notch service for the upscale visitor without charging much more than neighboring Park City or The Canyons. The higher price guarantees short lift lines, enforced slow ski areas and personal attention throughout your stay. You might even rub shoulders with ski legend Stein Eriksen, Deer Valley's Director of Skiing.

While the resort has two main entrances, families should stick to the Snow Park Base Area. Ambassadors will help you load and unload your skis. Inside the expansive day lodge, you'll find everything your family needs. Lockers, basket service and rental equipment are located downstairs, while complimentary ski storage, a delicious (but expensive) buffet-style restaurant (with great breakfasts) and the resort's first-rate daycare facility (435-645-6648) are on the first floor. Kids who attend daycare hang out in style, as the facility has three floors of space to play

DEER VALLEY RESORT

CENTRAL LINE
800-424-DEER (3337) or 435-649-1000

CENTRAL RESERVATION LINE
800-558-DEER (3337)

SNOW REPORT
435-649-2000

ANNUAL SNOWFALL
300 inches.

INFORMATION
www.deervalley.com

SEASON
Early Dec—mid-April.

HOURS
Daily, 9 am—4:15 pm.

in, and a low child-to-caretaker ratio that guarantees your tot tons of one-on-one time.

On the slopes, trails tend to be on the moderate side. Beginners and intermediate-level skiers make tracks on Bald Eagle Mountain. New to skiing? Ride the Snowflake or Burn lift to the separate, protected area called Wild West. It's the perfect place to find your edges. For some eye-popping vistas, try the runs off the Carpenter and Silver Lake Express high-speed quads. You'll get to meander past multi-million dollar homes as you cruise down the slopes. Try Bald Mountain or Flagstaff if you love glade skiing. Empire Canyon, Deer Valley's most remote terrain, runs the gamut from a mellow family ski area off Little Chief to double diamond shoots and bowls at the peak.

As the site of the 2002 Olympic slalom, mogul and aerial freestyle events, Deer Valley is investing millions of dollars in improvements. This is one resort your family will want to add to your list of favorite ski destinations.

◉ At a Glance

ADDRESS P.O. Box 1525, Park City, UT 84060.
LOCATION Northern Utah.
TERRAIN MIX 4 mountains, 1,750 acres.
VERTICAL 3,000 feet (**PEAK** 9,570 feet. **BASE** 6,570 feet).
TRAILS 88 (15% Beginner, 50% Advanced, 35% Expert).
LIFTS 20 (1 gondola, 5 high-speed quads, 3 quads, 8 triples, 2 doubles, 1 magic carpet).
DAILY LIFT TICKET RATES (US) Adults $63, seniors (over 64) $44, children (under 13) $34.
SNOWMAKING 29%.
NIGHT SKIING None.
ACTIVITIES Nordic skiing, ice-skating, dog sledding, snowmobiling. Park City (1 mile away) has plenty of activities.
BABYSITTERS 435-645-6612.
DAYCARE Children's Center, daily, 8:30 am—4:30 pm, 2 months to 12 years, reservations recommended (888-754 8477 or 435-645-6612).
CHILDREN'S LESSONS AND CAMPS Ski School (888-754-8477 or 435-645-6612).
HOSPITAL Park City Family Health & Emergency Clinic (435-649-7640).
SPECIAL DEALS Utah Passport, multi-resort lift ticket offer for international guests.
SPECIAL PROGRAMS Complimentary pager service, free intermediate and expert mountain host tours, free overnight ski storage, specialty clinics.
GOOD MEETING PLACES Snow Park Lodge (base), Empire Canyon Lodge (on-slope), Silver Lake Lodge (on-slope).
DISTANCES IN MILES Denver, CO 546; Salt Lake City, UT 36.

Snowbird

Situated on the western slopes of Wasatch Range, Snowbird is only 25 miles from Salt Lake City and a short drive from the international airport. Less travel means more time on the trails enjoying the massive quantities of powder, exploring the highly-developed base area and experiencing the excellent off-slope amenities.

The Family Channel awarded Snowbird the Seal of Quality because of its can't-be-beat ski and ride free program for children under 12 (two per paying adult). The resort also boasts impressive instructional programs. Over 320 ski and snowboard instructors and expansive slope-side facilities offer children a terrific learning environment. Mountain School ski weeks are full of creative activities and kids enrolled in the program always get a thrill out of the Cookie Duel races every Thursday.

First-timers in your family? Head to Gad Valley base area, just downhill from Snowbird Center and Cliff Lodge. Here you can coast down the family ski zones and interpretive Ske-cology trails. Make sure to check out the Kid's Park Mining Town replica just off Bluebell run. The ski-through figures are a big hit with youngsters.

SNOWBIRD
CENTRAL LINE 801-933-2222
CENTRAL RESERVATION LINE 800-453-3000
SNOW REPORT 801-933-2100
INFORMATION www.snowbird.com
ANNUAL SNOWFALL 500 inches.
SEASON Mid-Nov—late May.
HOURS Daily, 9 am—4:30 pm (until 8:30 pm on Wed and Fri).

There's lots of terrain for intermediates and experts. With the Mineral Basin addition in 2000, the resort has grown by almost 20 percent. Whether you choose blue, black or double diamond, top-to-bottom runs are lengthy and views are second to none. While the tram offers a warm ride up, if you want to save money, purchase chairlift-only passes that access the entire mountain at a fraction of the full price.

Snowbird's non-skiing activities include ice-skating, night-time tubing near the Cliff Lodge and evening lugeing on Chickadee slope. Look to the Activity Center (in Snowbird Ultimate Mountain Outfitters in the Plaza) for a complete list of après-ski options. Or call the resort's event hotline (801-933-2110). For indoor fun, check out Snowbird's signature accommodation. Part hotel, part condo and part cruise ship, Cliff Lodge (801-742-2222) offers licensed childcare, ski-in, ski-out access, ski equipment and rentals. The facility also provides ski movies, a variety of virtual reality and video games, plus a games room with pool tables and air hockey. There are four restaurants (all serve kid-fare), three lounges, a business center and numerous shops to browse. The Lodge also has a first-rate spa, offering parents an unbelievable selection of treatments. You can luxuriate while the kids are well taken care of—the Lodge serves up Kid's Club evening parties to keep little tykes entertained.

👁 At a Glance

ADDRESS   Little Cotton Canyon Road, Snowbird, Utah 84092.
LOCATION   Northern Utah.
TERRAIN MIX   2 mountains, 2,500 acres.
VERTICAL   3,240 feet (**PEAK** 11,000 feet. **BASE** 7,760 feet).
TRAILS   82 (25% Beginner, 35% Advanced, 40% Expert).
LIFTS   13 (a 125-person tram, 4 high-speed quads, 6 doubles, 2 surface tows).
DAILY LIFT TICKETS RATES (US)   Ticket rates based on lifts used: Adults; tram $56, chairlifts only $47. Seniors (65 to 69); tram $41, chairlifts only $32. Seniors (over 69); tram $27, chairlifts only $22.50. Children under 13 free (two per paying adult).
NIGHT SKIING TICKET RATES   Flat rate $10.
SNOWMAKING   100 acres.
NIGHT SKIING   Chickadee lift beginner area, one run, 142 vertical feet.
ACTIVITIES   Tubing, lugeing (801-933-2147), ice-skating, snowshoeing, helicopter skiing (801-742-2800), Cliff spa, live jazz, adventure lecture series, ski movies.
BABYSITTERS   48-hour notification required (801-933-2256).
DAYCARE   Camp Snowbird, daily, 8:30 am—4:30 pm, 6 weeks to 12 years (801-933-2256).
CHILDREN'S LESSONS AND CAMPS   Camp Snowbird, Wings for Teens (holiday weeks only), (801-933-2256).
HOSPITAL   Alta View Hospital (801-501-2231).
SPECIAL DEALS   Smith's Food and Drug grocery offers discount tickets.
SPECIAL PROGRAMS   Women's Snowboard Camps, Silverwings (skiers over 50), Snowboard Steeps & Half Pipe Camps, Ski Steeps Camps.
GOOD MEETING PLACES   Snowbird Plaza Deck.
GETTING AROUND   Canyon Transportation Van Service (800-225-1841), Utah Transit Authority (801-287-4636).
DISTANCES IN MILES   Denver, CO 545; Salt Lake City, UT 25.

CHAPTER THREE

Colorado and New Mexico

Colorado's mountains have long been delighting snow lovers the world over and account for 20 percent of the total annual ski visits in the United States. From Vail's five-star resorts to the mountain-top oasis in Durango, there's something for everyone in Colorado. You are guaranteed to find excellent value for you destination dollar, particularly in the highly competitive market near Denver.

At Vail Resorts (Vail, Beaver Creek, Breckenridge and Keystone) you'll find just about every possible amenity and plenty of fun activities just for kids. Nearby, Copper serves up competitive prices with its new pedestrian village, imaginative daycare and a renown ski and boarding school. Winter Park, owned by the city of Denver, boasts huge terrain and excellent children's facilities, complimented by an unparalleled adaptive skiing program for disabled skiers.

The massive terrain (four mountains) at Aspen & Snowmass coupled with a friendly pedestrian village provides a unique family vacation getaway. Looking for big snowfall? Head north to Steamboat in Ski Town USA. This mammoth-sized ski area offers everything from a superb one-stop children's vacation center to the legendary Champagne Powder™ glades.

Southwest of Denver, Crested Butte offers brilliant vistas, great children's programming and a slope-side Club Med. Telluride has several villages and first-class, first-rate children's services. Nighttime programs include skiing, snow toy riding and lots indoor fun in a central mid-mountain location. Durango, located further south, offers a smaller-scale resort with short lift lines and a single central base area. Taos is the classic skiers-only resort in New Mexico. Expect old-style skiing, exceptional instruction, gorgeous views and quiet nights.

0   50   100   250 miles

0 50 100   200   350 km

Colorado and New Mexico

Colorado
★ Aspen & Snowmass
★ Beaver Creek & Vail
★ Copper Mountain
★ Crested Butte
★ Durango
★ Steamboat
★ Telluride
★ Winter Park

New Mexico
★ Taos Ski Valley

COLORADO

Aspen & Snowmass

Families making the trek to the four snow-topped peaks of Aspen are in for a treat. Aspen is much more than a resort. It has four separate ski areas (Aspen Mountain, Aspen Highlands, Buttermilk and Snowmass) with a combined 4,800 acres of ski-able terrain spread over 12 miles. Furthermore, it boasts a lively town complete with over 100 restaurants and bars, incredible art galleries, fun family activities and shopping galore.

Although there are wealthy people skiing and living in Aspen, it's possible for your family to enjoy it without spending a fortune. Brown bagging is still in vogue with plenty of picnic tables available. There are also many amenities that most mountains don't offer, including complimentary on-slope water, apple cider, coffee and tissue stations. At the end of the day, Aspen village serves up free cider and cookies for all.

Families looking for a sitter should contact Aspen Babysitting Company (970-948-6849). For daycare, call Aspen Daycare (970-925-3136) or Snowmass' Snow Clubs (970-923-1227). There's even Nighthawks evening childcare for three to ten year-olds. Have tots who want to ski? Sign them up for the multi-lingual, first-class Ski and Snowboard School of Aspen. With bases at each mountain, there are enough programs to suit every level. Kids up to four years old ski with the Big Burn Bears and five to six year-olds can join the Grizzlies. There is also a Too Cool for School teen program and backcountry guide service for experts. Everyone loves the Beginner's

ASPEN MOUNTAIN

CENTRAL LINE
800-525-6200

CENTRAL RESERVATION LINE
800-290-1327
or 970-925-9000

SNOW REPORT
970-925-1221
or 888-277-3676

ANNUAL SNOWFALL
300 inches.

INFORMATION
www.aspensnowmass.com
or www.stayaspen.com

SEASON
Mid-Nov—late April.

HOURS
Daily, 9 am—4 pm.

Magic program and race days. Youngsters get a kick out of the on-slope mascots, forts and special kids-only trails. If you're looking for powder, sign up for First Tracks—it's offered daily at Aspen Mountain and Wednesdays and Fridays at Snowmass (800-525-6200).

Each of the mountains offers a different experience. Aspen Mountain features intermediate and expert slopes for skiers and boarders. The terrain is famous for its short steeps and big bumps. Keep your eye out for Aspen's slope-side shrines to Elvis Presley, Jerry Garcia, Marilyn Monroe and John Denver.

Highlands is the locals' favorite spot to ski. It covers the range of beginner to expert trails, but hard-core skiers and boarders stick to the double diamond steeps in Highland Bowl. A Snowcat service brings you from Lodge Meadow to the top of Whip's Veneration, shortening the hike to the mountain's 12,500-foot peak. An advanced lift system rockets riders to the top of the mountain, while a recently completed village serves up great après-ski activities.

Have beginners in your crew? Stop at Buttermilk and ski the gently sloping wide-open runs. These easy slopes help newbies gain confidence. Try the popular terrain park and half pipe for more advanced skiers and boarders. If you need to burn more energy, join the locals and snowshoe up Buttermilk when there's a full moon.

SNOWMASS
CENTRAL LINE
800-525-6200
or 970-923-1220
CENTRAL RESERVATION LINE
800-598-2005
SNOW REPORT
970-925-1221
ANNUAL SNOWFALL
300 inches.
INFORMATION
www.aspensnowmass.com or
www.snowmassvillage.com
SEASON
Mid-Nov—late April.
HOURS
Daily, 9 am—4 pm.

Snowmass offers the longest lift-serviced vertical in the U.S.—4,406 feet—with over 3,000 acres of cruisers, steeps and snowboard parks. It comes with 95 percent ski-in ski-out accommodation and a lively pedestrian village. Bring the brood to the Family Zone. Accessible from the Burlingame lift, right off Snowmass Village Mall, it's filled with kids' trails, a terrain park and at the end of Rudolph's Run, there are reindeer to visit. Kids love the treed trails, such as King Louie's Traverse, Pinball Alley and Lizard Lane. When the sun sets and you still want more, race down Tube Town's descents, located on Assay Hill ($15).

For off-slope excitement, head to Aspen Center for Environmental Studies (970-925-5756). You can snowshoe with naturalists or listen to educational slide shows and talks. There's also dog sledding, hot air ballooning, sleigh rides and ice-skating at Silver Circle. If your kids want to do something special, check out the array of evening programs, including movie nights, nature evenings, storytelling and BBQs (970-925-1220). For one-stop accommodation shopping, call 800-290-1327 or 800-SNOW-MASS. No matter where you stay, a free shuttle bus services the valley.

👁 At a Glance

ASPEN MOUNTAIN

ADDRESS P.O. Box 1248, Aspen, CO 81612.

LOCATION Central Colorado.

TERRAIN MIX 1 mountain, 673 acres.

VERTICAL 3,267 feet (**PEAK** 11,212 feet. **BASE** 7,945 feet).

TRAILS 76 (35% Intermediate, 35% Advanced, 30% Expert).

LIFTS 8 (6 person gondola, 1 high-speed quad, 2 quads, 1 high-speed double, 3 doubles).

DAILY LIFT TICKET RATES (US) Adults $65, youths (13 to 17) $51, children (7 to 12) $41, under 7 free.

SNOWMAKING 30% (210 acres).

NIGHT SKIING None.

ACTIVITIES Alpine guides, Aspen Club & Spa, Nordic skiing, dog sledding, campfire storytelling, horse-drawn sleigh rides, hot air ballooning, ice-skating, Snowcat dinners, snowmobiling, sledding, snowshoeing, Winter Wild Things (970-925-5756), gallery tours, paragliding.

BABYSITTERS Aspen Babysitting Company (970-948-6849).

DAYCARE Aspen Daycare, daily, 8:30 am—4:30 pm (970-925-3136).

CHILDREN'S LESSONS AND CAMPS Ski & Snowboard Schools of Aspen, Too Cool for School (800-AT-ASPEN or 970-923-1227).

HOSPITAL Aspen Valley Hospital (970-925-1120).

SPECIAL DEALS Seniors (over 69) can save with a Silver Pass ($99). Seasonal specials available at www.aspensnowmass.com

SPECIAL PROGRAMS First Tracks, guiding, Hut to Hut adventures, Beginner's Magic Ski School programs, powder tours.

GOOD MEETING PLACES The Sundeck (top of gondola), gondola base.

DISTANCES IN MILES Denver, CO 220; Grand Junction, CO 125; Salt Lake City, UT 410.

SNOWMASS

ADDRESS   P.O. Box 1248, Aspen, CO 81612.

LOCATION   Central Colorado.

TERRAIN MIX   3 mountain faces, 3,010 acres.

VERTICAL   4,406 feet (**PEAK** 12,510 feet. **BASE** 8,104 feet).

TRAILS   83 (7% Beginner, 55% Intermediate, 18% Advanced, 20% Expert).

LIFTS   20 (7 high-speed quads, 3 triples, 5 doubles, 3 surface, 2 magic carpets).

DAILY LIFT TICKET RATES (US)   Adults $65, youths (13 to 17) $51, children (7 to 12) $41, under 7 free.

SNOWMAKING   5% (180 acres).

NIGHT SKIING   None.

ACTIVITIES   Tube Town (until 8 pm), storytelling, movie nights, nature evenings (970-925-5756), Alpine guides, Aspen Club & Spa, Nordic skiing, dog sledding, campfire storytelling, horse-drawn sleigh rides, hot air ballooning, ice-skating, Snowcat dinners, snowmobiling, sledding, snowshoeing, Winter Wild Things (970-925-5756), gallery tours, paragliding.

BABYSITTERS   Aspen Babysitting Company (970-948-6849).

DAYCARE   Snow Clubs, daily, 8:30 am — 4 pm (970-923-1227). Nighthawks Childcare (970-925-1220).

CHILDREN'S LESSONS AND CAMPS   Ski & Snowboard Schools of Aspen (800-AT-ASPEN or 970-923-1227).

HOSPITAL   Aspen Valley Hospital (970-925-1120).

SPECIAL DEALS   For seasonal specials, visit www.aspensnowmass.com

SPECIAL PROGRAMS   First tracks, guiding, Hut to Hut adventures, Beginner's Magic Ski School programs, powder tours.

GOOD MEETING PLACES   Snowmass Village Mall (base), Lynn Britt Cabin (mid-mountain).

DISTANCES IN MILES   Denver, CO 220; Grand Junction, CO 125; Salt Lake City, UT 410.

Beaver Creek & Vail

Vail and Beaver Creek, two of the ski industry's most famous mountains, are situated nine miles apart and are known collectively (with sister resorts Breckenridge and Keystone) as the Vail Resorts. Combined, they make a fabulous vacation spot for ski families. Vail contains the largest single mountain ski area in North America, while Beaver Creek offers a more discerning, upscale experience. With more than 100 restaurants, tons of kid-friendly activities, a ski museum and nearly 7,000 acres of skiable terrain, everyone is sure to have a great time.

Families with toddlers can take them to the Small World Play School daycare. It's an open and colorful facility with locations at both mountains. In Vail, it's located in the Golden Peak base area (970-479-3285). You'll find it in the Main Village at Beaver Creek (970-845-5325). If you need to suit up, you can purchase all the gear you need for the younger folk. Children who want to learn and adults looking to improve should register with the Vail and Beaver Creek Ski and Snowboard Schools. They offer a range of classes from beginner, full-day adventure packages to private lessons and backcountry guides. Disabled skiers can ride with PSIA/Adaptive Certified or Disabled Sports instructors.

Make sure everyone in the family has a map of all four Vail Resorts areas. The terrain is immense and meeting up can be difficult unless you plan ahead. Kids skiing on their own should pick up the Kids' Adventure Zone map at the ski school locations. It outlines out-of-the-way spots that include forts, jumps and secret parks in the woods. When lunchtime rolls around, head to Chaos Canyon Kids' Café at the terrace level at Mid-Vail. This restaurant offers a kid-specific menu and is decorated and designed for kids (adult-fare is served too).

Beginners can work their turns off almost every chair on Vail's face because of readily accessible green runs and catwalks. Once you hit Vail's legendary back bowls however, it's entirely intermediate and expert-level skiing. Powder hounds looking for an even bigger thrill can try Blue Sky Basin's 645 acres of backcountry terrain.

If you're looking for bumps, hit Beaver Creek's Grouse Mountain. Ski the intermediates at Beaver Creek and enjoy the classic boulevard cruising on the World Cup venue, Birds of Prey. Beaver Creek has easier terrain off most of its lifts and a unique beginner-only area at the top of the mountain. Keep

BEAVER CREEK

CENTRAL LINE
970-845-9090

CENTRAL RESERVATION LINE
800-404-3535
or 970-496-6772

SNOW REPORT
970-476-4888

ANNUAL SNOWFALL
331 inches.

INFORMATION
www.snow.com or
www.beavercreek.com

SEASON
Mid-Nov—mid-April.

HOURS
Daily, 8:30 am—4 pm.

VAIL

CENTRAL LINE
970-476-9090

CENTRAL RESERVATION LINE
800-404-3535
or 970-496-6772

SNOW REPORT
970-476-4888

ANNUAL SNOWFALL
346 inches.

INFORMATION
www.snow.com or
www.vail.com

SEASON
Mid-Nov—late April.

HOURS
Daily, 8:30 am—4 pm.

in mind that it boasts over 4,000 feet of vertical, which means a long way down for beginners. If you have Nordic skiers in your crew, McCoy Park atop Beaver Creek features 20 miles of tracked and untracked terrain.

After hours, Vail Valley delivers everything from dog sledding to fireworks, and horseback riding to ice-skating. Got energy to burn? Head to Adventure Ridge, Vail's winter wonderland. Ride the Eagle Bahn gondola and go snowmobiling (kid-sized machines available), play a round of laser tag, try snow biking, tubing or thrill sledding. Reservations are required (970-476-9090 or 970-479-4380 after 5 pm). You can rock climb at the Vail Mountain Lodge & Spa or head to the Colorado Ski Museum to peruse relics of this age-old sport. If you'd rather do something relaxing, visit the Vail Public Library and pick up some books. For details about these and other activities, contact the Activities Desk (970-476-9090).

Especially for kids (6 to 12), Vail's Night Owl program runs two days a week at the Children's Ski and Snowboard Center (4:30 pm to 8:30 pm). At Beaver Creek, children (5 to 12) get a night out Western-style, featuring western music, a wagon wheel pizza dinner, storytelling and an entertaining show from 6 pm to 9 pm. Moms and Dads can catch some time alone on the sleigh ride dinner to Beano's Cabin at Beaver Creek, or Game Creek at Vail. For more options, contact the Beaver Creek family adventure line (970-478-4090) or the concierge (970-479-4090).

Although a resort of this size can be expensive, there are ways for families to save money. Since competition is fierce amongst the Denver-vicinity ski hills, early season and spring tend to be quite affordable. And with the recent expansion of flights arriving at the local Vail/Eagle airport, getting here has never been easier. Vail Resort's multi-day tickets are transferable to all resorts, (including Keystone, Breckenridge and Arapahoe Basin), so you can ski any of the five resorts anytime.

Vail has accommodations to fit every taste. Call the reservation line (800-270-4870) or visit www.vail.com for details. If you are staying in Beaver Creek or want good access to both resorts, try the spacious one to three bedroom condos at Beaver Creek West (970-949-4840; www.beavercreekwest.com). It's located on the shuttle line, so you can leave your car parked throughout your stay.

◉ At a Glance

BEAVER CREEK

ADDRESS P.O. Box 7, Vail, CO 81658.

LOCATION 2 hours west of Denver.

TERRAIN MIX 3 mountains, 1,625 acres.

VERTICAL 4,040 feet (**PEAK** 11,440 feet. **BASE** 7,400 feet).

TRAILS 146 (34% Beginner, 39% Intermediate, 27% Expert).

LIFTS 16 (6 high-speed quads, 3 triples, 4 doubles, 3 magic carpets).

DAILY LIFT TICKET RATES (US) Adults $63, seniors (65 to 69) $55, seniors (over 69) $35, children (5 to 12) $39, under 5 free.

SNOWMAKING 580 acres.

NIGHT SKIING None.

ACTIVITIES Thursday Night Lights, star gazing, Movie night at the Villar Center, Kids Night Out, Figure Skating Series, Performance Art at the Villar Center, snowshoeing and Nordic skiing at McCoy Park, cooking classes, spas, yoga, aerobics, tennis, fly fishing, ice-skating, telemark skiing.

BABYSITTERS Small World Play School (970-845-5325).

DAYCARE Small World Play School, daily, 8 am — 4:30 pm, 2 months to 6 years (970-845-5325).

CHILDREN'S LESSONS AND CAMPS Beaver Creek Ski & Snowboard School (970-845-5464).

HOSPITAL Vail Valley Medical Center (970-476-2451).

SPECIAL DEALS Visit www.snow.com for specials.

SPECIAL PROGRAMS Snowshoeing and Nordic Skiing clinics and tours at McCoy Park, Racing Clinics, Her Turn, Hyatt Technique Weeks, Mountain Welcome Tours, Ski Valet.

GOOD MEETING PLACES Spruce Saddle, Red Tail Camp, Rendezvous Bar & Grill.

GETTING AROUND Intra-city bus, daily, 5 am — 2:30 am. Avon/Beaver Creek Transit provides bus service from Vail to Beaver Creek. Vail Resorts Express provides chartered shuttle service to Keystone and Breckenridge.

DISTANCES IN MILES Albuquerque, NM 540; Denver International Airport, CO 130; Salt Lake City, UT 430; Vail/Eagle County Airport, CO 25.

VAIL

ADDRESS P.O. Box 7, Vail, CO 81658.

LOCATION 2 hours west of Denver.

TERRAIN MIX Front side, Back bowls, Blue-Sky Basin, 5,289 acres.

VERTICAL 3,450 feet (**PEAK** 11,570 feet. **BASE** 8120 feet).

TRAILS 193 (18% Beginner, 29% Intermediate, 53% Expert).

LIFTS 33 (1 gondola, 14 high-speed quads, 1 quad, 3 triples, 5 doubles, 9 surface).

DAILY LIFT TICKET RATES (US) Adults $63, seniors (65 to 69) $55, seniors (over 69) $35, children (5 to 12) $39, under 5 free.

SNOWMAKING 380 acres.

NIGHT SKIING None.

ACTIVITIES Adventure Ridge (sledding, tubing, ski-biking, ice-skating, snowmobiling, Laser Tag), Night Owl children's program, movie theaters, live performances, fireworks, Nordic skiing, snowshoeing, telemark skiing, spa, fly fishing.

BABYSITTERS   Mountain Sitters (970-477-0024), Mount'n Munchkins (970-524-0309).

DAYCARE   Small World Play School, daily, 8 am—4:30 pm, 2 months to 6 years (970-479-3285).

CHILDREN'S LESSONS AND CAMPS   Vail Ski & Snowboard School (970-479-3280).

HOSPITAL   Vail Valley Medical Center (970-476-2451).

SPECIAL DEALS   Check www.snow.com for specials.

SPECIAL PROGRAMS   Adaptive programs, Nordic programs, 3-day Her Turn workshops, Pepi's Wedel Weeks, free daily Mountain Tours.

GOOD MEETING PLACES   Two Elk Restaurant (mid-mountain), Eagles Nest, (top of chair 11), Mid-Vail.

GETTING AROUND   Intra-city bus, daily, 5 am—2:30 am. Avon/Beaver Creek Transit provides bus service from Vail to Beaver Creek. Vail Resorts Express provides chartered shuttle service to Keystone and Breckenridge.

DISTANCES IN MILES   Albuquerque, NM 540; Denver International Airport, CO 120; Salt Lake City, UT 430; Vail/Eagle County Airport, CO 35.

Copper Mountain

Take a mountain famous for its excellent fall lines, thrill-inducing vertical, local appeal and family-friendly feel; spend $500 million on improvements and what do you get? Copper Mountain—a modernized, luxurious, world-class resort with a wealth of on- and off-slope activities, amenities and trails to meet every skier's desire.

Families arriving at Copper Mountain have it easy. Head straight to the Mountain Adventure Center in Copper One Lodge, located in the New Village. It's a one-stop vacation shop, including rentals, retail, lift tickets, ski school sign up and a cafeteria to stock up on fuel before hitting the slopes. There are even specially designated family restrooms on the first floor so your brood can get ready in privacy.

For those new to the sport, start at Union Creek where the lower slopes are layered with magic carpets and surface lifts. As you and your kids gain confidence, make your way to the three chairlifts that access slightly more challenging terrain. If you need a break, head to The School House at Union Creek, which offers pint-sized facilities, from special bathrooms to small tables to a sizable kids' menu. For more skiing enjoyment, test out the American Flyer and Eagle lifts, located near the Adventure Center. They service groomed beginner and intermediate trails.

Advanced skiers will get into the groove on the high-speed Super Bee six-pack, while experts stick to the peak lifts and classic Colorado back bowls. For terrain park junkies, don't miss the recent additions to the Tsunami and Banzai Pipeline, as well as the kickers, spines and tabletops in Bouncer Terrain Park. No matter where you choose to ski during the day, when the lifts close everyone heads to Molly B's restaurant in the East Village to enjoy Moe Dixon's live show. Considered one of the best entertainers in the ski industry, Moe will have your whole family singing and dancing in no time.

The New Village is an excellent spot to relax and absorb the ski culture. Enjoy the pedestrian-only traffic as you sit in one of the cafés. Take in an outdoor concert, test your strength at Sumo wrestling (kids get a kick out of dressing up in oversized rubber suits to compete with other guests) or partake in one of the many activities in the open-air "Beach" area.

COPPER MOUNTAIN RESORT

CENTRAL LINE
800-458-8386
or 970-968-2882

CENTRAL RESERVATION LINE
888-263-5302

SNOW REPORT
800-789-7609
or 970-968-2100

ANNUAL SNOWFALL
280 inches.

INFORMATION
www.ski-copper.com

SEASON
Mid-Nov — mid-April.

HOURS
Daily, 9 am — 4 pm
(opens at 8:30 am on
weekends).

Looking for a night away from the kids? Copper Mountain has created an evening program from 5 pm to 10 pm to enable Mom and Dad to get out for dinner while those under 11 get a fun-filled night of games, kid-food and movies. Even better, the childcare is free, providing you spend $30 while shopping or dining at the resort. In-room babysitting is also available through the Belly Button Bakery Daycare (888-229-9474).

Recent improvements to Copper include a lift-accessed tubing hill, a climbing wall and an ice-skating rink. The resort renovations are far from over. In the coming years, look for a cabriolet-style gondola to transport skiers from the parking lots, as well as further improvements to snowmaking. With the new "zoned" trail map, families find it easier to ski together. Your troop will want to extend their trip a little longer to enjoy everything this resort has to offer.

👁 At a Glance

ADDRESS 209 Ten Mile Circle, P.O. Box 3001, Copper Mountain, CO 80443.

LOCATION Central Colorado.

TERRAIN MIX 3 peaks, 2,433 acres.

VERTICAL 2,601 feet (**PEAK** 12,313 feet. **BASE** 9,712 feet).

TRAILS 125 (21% Beginner, 25% Intermediate, 36% Advanced, 18% Expert).

LIFTS 23 (a 6-person high-speed lift, 4 high-speed quads, 5 triples, 5 doubles, 2 surface, 6 magic carpets).

DAILY LIFT TICKETS RATES (US) Adults $55, seniors (60 to 69) $39, children (6 to 13) $24, over 70 and under 6 free.

SNOWMAKING 16%.

NIGHT SKIING None.

ACTIVITIES Tubing, Dining in the Woods, Solitude by Starlight, snowshoeing, tubing, snowmobiling, sleigh rides, Nordic skiing, Racquet and Athletic Club, ice-skating, fly fishing, climbing wall, snow scooters, Kids' Night Out, Fire Side Storytelling.

BABYSITTERS Belly Button Bakery (970-968-2318 ext. 38102).

DAYCARE Belly Button Bakery, daily, 8:30 am—5 pm, 6 weeks to 4 years, reservations required (970-968-2318 ext. 38102).

CHILDREN'S LESSONS AND CAMPS Copper Ski and Snowboard School (800-458-8386).

HOSPITAL Copper Mountain Medical Center (970-968-2330).

SPECIAL DEALS Ticket deals early in season and spring, local supermarkets offer discount tickets, seasonal specials.

SPECIAL PROGRAMS NASTAR Ski Racing, free mountain tours, Women's Wednesday clinics.

GOOD MEETING PLACES Solitude Station (upper mountain), Grand Hall at Copper Station (East Village), Endo's Restaurant (New Village).

DISTANCES IN MILES Albuquerque, NM 530; Denver International Airport, CO 90; Salt Lake City, UT 450; Vail/Eagle County Airport, CO 50.

Crested Butte

Crested Butte's magnificent peak is a beacon to families who want to ski in Colorado, but prefer to avoid the crowds. Situated just 17 miles south of Aspen, travelers flying into Denver have to either buckle up for a five-hour drive or hop aboard one of the four daily flights to Gunnison, located 30 miles from the resort. The extra travel time is well worth it when you consider

Crested Butte is as inexpensive as they come. Families especially love the "pay your age" deal for children (5 to 16). Furthermore, since there are no blackout dates, your eight-year-old can ski all season long for $8 per day.

The mountain resort's Town Center is the hub for family-friendly activities. Pick up your lift tickets at the Gothic building. For Baby Bears and Cuddly Bears Daycare (970-349-2259), as well as the Kid's Ski and Snowboard Worlds, visit the Whetstone building located slope-side (it has drop-off parking around the front). Make sure your kids know to keep their eyes open for Bubba and Betty Bear. These larger-than-life mascots love to hang out near the Gothic patio.

Once you are ready to start go, every-one in the family will find terrain to suit his or her liking. Crested Butte has enough variety for adults to get a good workout, while kids feel safe and comfortable because the resort isn't too large. Ski terrain varies from magic carpet accessed beginner areas to the heart-stopping steeps atop the High lift. For serious thrill seekers, test out Headwall, the same trail on which the US Extreme Games is held each April. With the tougher terrain up high, less experienced skiers should stay closer to the base on the Keystone high-speed quad, Painter Boy and Peachtree chairs. Trek to groomed intermediate and advanced bowl skiing off the Paradise high-speed quad. If you want maximum vertical, there's a classic 20-minute hike that brings you to the top of the peak. Then it's a thigh-burning, 2.6-mile descent to the base of Treasury. For sun lovers, stick to the East River slopes in the morning, the front side around noon, and the Silver Queen high-speed quad later in the day.

Plan to stop at the on-slope Paradise Warming House or the Gothic Center Cafeteria at the base for lunch. Kick back and relax while the kids plan their evening activities. They can choose from a wide range of age-specific programs, as well as a Kid's Night Out on Saturdays from 6 pm to 10 pm. On Wednesdays,

CRESTED BUTTE MOUNTAIN RESORT

CENTRAL LINE
800-544-8448
or 970-349-2333

CENTRAL RESERVATION LINE
800-544-8448
or 970-349-2390

SNOW REPORT
888-44-BUTTE
(28883)

AVERAGE SNOWFALL
298 inches.

INFORMATION
www.crestedbutte
resort.com

SEASON
Mid-Dec — mid-April.

HOURS
Daily, 9 am — 4 pm.

youngsters can sign up for a torchlight dinner. After eating atop the mountain, they ski down using glow sticks to light their way.

A good distance from any major city, Crested Butte's status as "the last great Colorado ski town" still holds true. Elk Street's old-fashioned Victorian storefronts hearken back to the town's mining roots. The influx of small-scale real estate developments however, is giving the resort town a facelift. Plans also include revamping the Town Center and building a new ski school facility and lifts. The slope-side Club Med makes this resort a destination must for families. Its all-inclusive deals come complete with amazing activities and amenities for kids. For those looking for a more independent vacation, there are a number of local hotels, bed & breakfasts and condos that can be rented through the central reservation number (888-463-6714). No matter where you stay, the ski hill is only a seven-minute free shuttle ride from the old town. Crested Butte Mountain Resort is a guaranteed good time. Start packing. You don't want the kids to miss out on this ski vacation.

◉ At a Glance

ADDRESS 17 Emmons Loop, P.O. Box A, Mt. Crested Butte, CO 81225.
LOCATION South central Colorado.
TERRAIN MIX 1 mountain, 1,058 acres.
VERTICAL 2,775 feet (**PEAK** 12,162 feet. **BASE** 9,375 feet).
TRAILS 85 (15% Beginner, 44% Intermediate, 10% Advanced, 31% Expert).
LIFTS 14 (3 high-speed quads, 3 triples, 3 doubles, 3 surface, 2 magic carpets).
DAILY LIFT TICKET RATES (US) Adults $53, seniors (65 to 69) $27, children (5 to 16) pay their age, over 70 and under 5 ski free.
SNOWMAKING 20%.
NIGHT SKIING None.
ACTIVITIES Sleigh ride dinners, fondue parties, torchlight parades, snowshoeing, snowmobiling, ice-skating, horseback riding, dog sledding, ice fishing, ice-climbing.
BABYSITTERS Call the Sheraton Concierge (970-349-8015).
DAYCARE Kids' World, daily, 8:30 am — 4:30 pm, 6 months to 7 years (970-349-2259).
CHILDREN'S LESSONS AND CAMPS Kids' Ski and Snowboard World (970-349-2259).
HOSPITAL Gunnison County Hospital (970-641-1456).
SPECIAL DEALS Package deals (800-544-8448), free ski passes with lodging early and late in the season.
SPECIAL PROGRAMS Guided snowshoe tours, women's programs, Adaptive Sports Center activities (970-349-2296).

GOOD MEETING PLACES   Gothic Center Deck & Cafeteria (base), Paradise Warming House (on-slope).

GETTING AROUND   Mountain Express shuttle, daily, 7 am—midnight, free (between ski village and historic town).

DISTANCES IN MILES   Colorado Springs, CO 197; Denver, CO 231; Grand Junction, CO 158; Gunnison, CO 30.

Durango

This small-scale resort has made a big splash since Chuck Cobb took over in 1999. Formerly called Purgatory Resort, Durango Mountain Resort changed its name to strengthen ties with the historic mining town 30 miles down Highway 550. The ski hill and town of Durango offer a superb destination package for families with good skiing in tandem with shopping, art galleries, pubs, restaurants and a children's museum.

Recent renovations include a high-speed six-passenger super chair, improved accommodations and a slate of family programming —with more to come. The resort's 15-year development plan includes additional real estate, a new gondola and a mountaintop transfer lift from the face to Dante's backside restaurant.

Even without these changes, the mountain offers families two valuable things: moderate pricing and a simple layout. When you arrive, stop in at the Village Center, the only major base facility at Durango. Here you can store your brown bags and extra sweaters in coin-operated lockers. There are retail stores and rental shops offering standard and performance gear for skis, snowboards and skiboards. If you have tots who need care, head upstairs and drop them off at the resort's daycare facility (970-247-9000 ext. 144). Taking lessons? At Durango's Ski & Snowboard School learning is guaranteed. If you

DURANGO MOUNTAIN RESORT

CENTRAL LINE
800-525-0892
or 970-247-9000

CENTRAL RESERVATION LINE
800-525-0892

SNOW REPORT
970-247-9000

ANNUAL SNOWFALL
260 inches.

INFORMATION
www.durango
mountainresort.com

SEASON
Mid-Nov—early April.

HOURS
Daily, 9 am—4 pm.

don't think you've learned anything during your lesson, you get an additional lesson free.

On the slopes, expert trails flank the intermediate runs found in the middle of the mountain. Beginners have an oasis all to themselves, low and separate from the rest of the terrain. If you're a boarder, plan to spend the day at the resort's three terrain parks. Accessed from the Village six-pack chair, Pitchfork boasts a quarter-mile half pipe and rails, while Limbo has table tops and big air launchers. For Snag's open-style park with natural hills, headwalls and trees, head to the mountain's backside. Little skiers shouldn't miss Animas City Adventure Park. Named after a local ghost town, Animas City has old-fashioned ski-through storefronts and a kid-friendly glade.

Families take advantage of the quiet evenings and hop aboard the nightly Star Safaris, where you can peek through Colorado's largest privately owned telescope. Other family après-ski opportunities include dinner sleigh rides with Buck's Livery and a relaxing visit to Trimble Hot Springs for a soak and a massage, located just 20 minutes from Durango Mountain Resort. Call the central reservation number for information (900-979-9742).

If you're staying more than three days, the resort offers myriad non-ski activities interchangeable with your Total Adventure Ticket lift pass. Ride the Durango & Silverton Narrow Gauge Railroad to Cascade Canyon, or take the kids snowmobiling for the day. For a complete change in scenery, plan to visit the Children's Museum of Durango (970-259-9234), open Wednesday to Sunday. Stop halfway to town and watch bees make honey in Honeyville (800-676-7690).

A favorite ski haven for residents of Arizona, New Mexico and Texas, Durango's growth and change is starting to draw new visitors from around North America. With frequent flights to the local La Plate County Airport, more families are flocking to Durango and staying minutes from the hill at either Purgatory Village Condominium Hotel or East Rim Condominiums (800-693-0175).

◉ At a Glance

ADDRESS 1 Skier Place, Durango, Colorado 81301.
LOCATION Southwestern Colorado.
TERRAIN MIX 1 mountain, 1,200 acres.
VERTICAL 2,029 feet (**PEAK** 10,822 feet. **BASE** 8,793 feet).
TRAILS 75 (23% Beginner, 51% Advanced, 26% Expert).
LIFTS 11 (1 high-speed 6-pack, 1 high-speed quad, 4 triples, 3 doubles, 1 surface, 1 magic carpet).
DAILY LIFT TICKET RATES (US) Adults $50, seniors (62 to 69) $35, children (6 to 12) $25, over 69 and under 6 six free.
SNOWMAKING 20%.
NIGHT SKIING None.
ACTIVITIES Tubing, Tour the Universe Star Safaris, dinner sleigh rides, Nordic skiing, Trimble Hot Springs and Spa, Durango & Silverton Narrow Gauge Railroad, Snowcat skiing, snowmobile tours, snowshoe tours, Sky Ute Casino, fly fishing.
BABYSITTERS Funsitters (970-385-0299).
DAYCARE Cub Care, 2 months to 3 years, reservations required (970-385-2149).
CHILDREN'S LESSONS AND CAMPS Ski School (970-385-2149).
HOSPITAL Mercy Medical Center (970-247-4311).
SPECIAL DEALS Total Adventure Ticket (purchase a multi-day pass and exchange it for a non-ski activity day).
SPECIAL PROGRAMS Adaptive Sports Association, Guaranteed Ski School lessons, snow bike rentals and lessons.
GOOD MEETING PLACES Purgy's restaurant (base), Dante's (on-slope, backside).
DISTANCES IN MILES Albuquerque, NM 240; Denver, CO 300; Durango, CO 30; Telluride, CO 130.

Steamboat

It's no surprise that Ski Town USA is a popular destination for families from all over the globe. More than just world-class skiing, Steamboat boasts a vibrant village, excellent base area and huge terrain that continues to draw snow-lovers year after year. Best of all, powder hounds get their fix with some of the fluffiest desert-dry powder blanketing the slopes all season long.

Steamboat has made skiing with kids easy, thanks to the one-stop check-in counter at the Kids' Vacation Center, where parents can purchase lift tickets, rent equipment and sign up children for lessons. The daycare facilities (970-879-6111 ext. 469) are first-rate, including colorful rooms with plenty of games. The staff is friendly too, so parents feel comfortable leaving their kids (pagers are available for a nominal fee). If you'd rather try before you buy, visit the Open House Night every Saturday from 5 pm to 6 pm.

Need lessons yourself? Sign up for Steamboat's Perfect Turn Ski and Snow-board School (970-879-6111) and learn from one of their 300 pros. Beginners start at the recently reshaped Learn to Ski and Ride terrain near the base area. It's the perfect spot to test out your edges with a vast network of magic carpet and beginner lifts. Feeling confident? Ride the three-mile-long Why Not? run.

Advanced skiers have myriad possibilities. Join the First Tracks program and trek through Steamboat's legendary powder. The gladed areas off Pioneer Ridge, Sunshine and Storm Peak are this mountain's claim to fame. Amongst these treed runs, the term Champagne Powder™ was coined. Boarders should start at Dude Ranch terrain park, which contains a competition half pipe, then head over to Maverick, the big air park. Kids can test out mini-hits at Beehive in Rough Rider. If your family is looking to carve together, try the three intermediate family zones: Tomahawk, Flintlock and Bashor. Giggle Gulch and Swinger slow skiing areas are located on green terrain.

Lunch at Thunderhead, top of the Steamboat gondola. Kids' menus are available at Hazie's, or drop by the B.K. Corrall for cafeteria-style dining. Their buffet breakfast is a great deal—all-you-can-eat for $9, kids under 12 eat free.

When the sun sets, the pedestrian village comes alive. The Kids Adventure Club (970-879-6111 ext. 5375) operates nightly from Tuesday to Friday and offers an array of age-specific activities, from juggling to climbing to watching videos (pizza and ice cream sundaes served nightly). While the kids are playing, parents can eat at Hazie's or Ragnar's restaurant, or enjoy stand up comedy at the Bear River Bar & Grill. If you're looking for family fun, go tubing together at the base of the Headwall lift.

STEAMBOAT SKI AND RESORT CORPORATION

CENTRAL LINE
970-879-6111

CENTRAL RESERVATION LINE
800-922-2722

SNOW REPORT
970-879-7300

ANNUAL SNOWFALL
363 inches.

INFORMATION
www.steamboat.com

SEASON
Mid-Nov—mid-April.

HOURS
Daily, 8:30 am—4 pm.

There are plenty of lodging options, including the slope-side Bear Claw Condos (800-BEAR-CLAW) and the luxury Steamboat Grand Resort Hotel (877-269-2628). Call Steamboat Central Reservations™ (800-922-2722) or go online at www.steamboat.com for more options. Steamboat has been serving up family ski adventures since 1963, so no matter where you stay, you're guaranteed a good time.

👁 At a Glance

ADDRESS 2305 Mt. Werner Circle, Steamboat Springs, CO 80487.

LOCATION Northwestern Colorado.

TERRAIN MIX 6 mountains, 2,939 acres.

VERTICAL 3,668 feet (**PEAK** 10,568 feet. **BASE** 6,900 feet).

TRAILS 142 (13% Beginner, 56% Advanced, 31% Expert).

LIFTS 24 (an 8-person gondola, 4 high-speed quads, 1 quad, 6 triples, 6 doubles, 2 surface, 4 magic carpets).

DAILY LIFT TICKET RATES IN (US) Adults $52, seniors (65 to 69) $33, children (under 13) $29, over 70 free.

SNOWMAKING 15%.

NIGHT SKIING None.

ACTIVITIES Kids' Adventure Club, tubing, sleigh-ride dinners, Nordic skiing, dog sledding, ice-climbing, hot springs, fly fishing, ice-skating, snowshoeing, fitness center, winter driving school.

BABYSITTERS Kiddie Corral Childcare (970-879-6111 ext. 469).

DAYCARE Kiddie Corral Childcare, daily, 8:15 am—4:30 pm, 6 months to 6 years (970-879-6111 ext. 469).

CHILDREN'S LESSONS AND CAMPS Kids' Vacation Center, Teen Challenge, Desperados Ski Weeks (weekly group sessions), (970-879-6111 ext. 218 or 531).

HOSPITAL Yampa Valley Medical Center (970-879-1322).

SPECIAL DEALS Kids Ski Free™ (children ski free with adult 5-day passes), seasonal specials.

SPECIAL PROGRAMS Adaptive skiers, First Tracks, women's ski seminars, NASTAR racing, Billy Kidd Performance Center.

GOOD MEETING PLACES Express OH! (base area), Thunderhead Meeting Area (Steamboat gondola).

GETTING AROUND Free daily shuttle during ski hours.

DISTANCES IN MILES Denver, CO 180; Salt Lake City, UT 325.

Telluride

Telluride's got it all. Tucked into one of the most breath-taking alpine areas in the continental US, this quaint Victorian town comes equipped with varied ski terrain, cozy charm and plenty of amenities for families. Its free shuttle and gondola service transports guests to and from the historic town of Telluride to the Mountain Village. And believe it or not, this fantastic family vacation getaway is about to get better.

The resort has plans to erect three high-speed quads in Prospect Bowl, opening more mountaintop intermediate and beginner terrain. Telluride is also building an on-slope day lodge at the top of Lift 10. Families with inexperienced skiers won't just be relegated to the lower slopes. Instead, rookies and pros alike can enjoy the beauty of 13 and 14 thousand-foot peaks from the same vantage point.

> **TELLURIDE**
>
> **CENTRAL LINE**
>   800-801-4832
>   or 970-728-6900
>
> **CENTRAL LODGING**
>   800-854-3062
>
> **SNOW REPORT**
>   970-728-7425
>
> **ANNUAL SNOWFALL**
>   311 inches.
>
> **INFORMATION**
>   www.telluride-ski.com or
>   www.telluridekids.com
>
> **SEASON**
>   Late Nov—mid-April.
>
> **HOURS**
>   Daily, 8:45 am—4 pm.

During the day, Mountain Village is the place for families. It houses the ski school, guest services, retail and rental shops, overnight ski storage and the brightly lit Children's Center nursery (800-801-4832). For non-skiers, visit the Telluride Outside kiosk for a plethora of on- and off-slope fun. Once everyone is suited up, ride the magic carpet lift right outside the door to ease onto the slopes. The lifts closest to Mountain Village cater to beginners and intermediates. Daredevils should hit the Surge Air Garden terrain park, complete with several tabletops and a half pipe. For the best photo opportunities, take the lifts to the top and ski down the appropriately named blue run, See Forever.

If your kids are in ski school, they'll participate in a unique program that teaches local history while improving their turns. Classes are divided into Utes and Miners (ages 3 to 6) and Explorers (ages 7 to 12). Each day there's a different theme, including the environment, history and heritage, and safety on the slopes. Throughout the week, children enjoy presentations on the daily theme during lunch at Big Billies, the ski school dining area at the base of the Chondola (a half-quad, half-gondola) lift.

Mountain Village, the hub of evening activity at the resort, offers lift accessed tubing and tobogganing, snow-biking, ice-skating and a NASTAR racing course. There's an indoor video arcade and plenty of kid-food (pizza, hot dogs and hot chocolate) available. When your tykes are tuckered out, hop on the gondola and ride it back to the lodge, free of charge. Telluride offers a Kid's Night Out and Mystery Theater from 5:30 pm to 9 pm, once a week during peak season.

For in-town entertainment, families can eat at one of the kid-favorites: Fat Alley BBQ, Smuggler's Brew Pub or Color Me Mine, a paint-your-own ceramics café. There's a Youth Center (970-728-0140) for teens with daily and night programs, basketball and an in-line skating course. Visit the high school's indoor climbing wall ($5 per person), the outdoor ice-skating rink, the movie theater or the municipal library (970-728-6613), which serves up a variety of children's programs.

Telluride's remote locale caters to the avid ski family. Resort-Quest International offers the most complete assortment of accommodation in town. Through their central phone number (970-728-6621) or on-line at www.resortquest.com, you can reserve anything from a five-bedroom home in the town of Telluride to a quaint hotel or condo unit up in Mountain Village.

👁 At a Glance

ADDRESS   565 Mountain Village Boulevard, Telluride, CO 81435.
LOCATION   Southwestern Colorado.
TERRAIN MIX   1 mountain, 1,700 acres.
VERTICAL   3,535 feet (**PEAK** 12,260 feet. **BASE** 8,725 feet).
TRAILS   80 (22% Beginner, 38% Intermediate, 40% Advanced/Expert).
LIFTS   15 (two 8-person gondolas, 7 high-speed quads, 2 triples, 2 doubles, 1 surface, 1 magic carpet).
DAILY LIFT TICKET RATES (US)   Adults $62, seniors (65 to 69) $42, children (6 to 12) $35, over 69 and under 6 free.
SNOWMAKING   15%.
NIGHT SKIING   Lift 2, Adventure Hill.
ACTIVITIES   Kids Night Out, Sheridan Opera House's Mystery Theater, snow-biking, tubing, sledding, torchlight parades, NASTAR race course, snowmobiling, sleigh rides, dog sledding, natural hot springs, hot air ballooning, ice-climbing, fly fishing, glider rides, heli-skiing, historic walking tours, horseback riding, ice-skating, paddle tennis, paragliding,

snowshoeing, Nordic skiing, climbing wall, movie theaters, racquetball, squash, yoga.

BABYSITTERS   Traveling Tots (970-728-6618).

DAYCARE   Telski Nursery & Childcare, daily, 8:30 am—4 pm, 2 months to 3 years, reservations required (970-728-7533).

CHILDREN'S LESSONS AND CAMPS   Children's Adventures (3 to 12) and Telski Nursery & Childcare (970-728-7533).

HOSPITAL   Telluride Medical Center (970-728-3848).

SPECIAL DEALS   Pre-purchase 14 days in advance and get special deals. Specialty Sports/Gart Sports offers discounts. Visit www.telluride-ski.com for details.

SPECIAL PROGRAMS   Children's Adventure Club (entertains kids before and after lessons), women's weeks, adaptive skiing, race camps.

GOOD MEETING PLACES   Gorrono Ranch (on-slope), top of Lift 10, Big Billies.

GETTING AROUND   Galloping Goose shuttle, daily, 7 am—11 pm, free. Gondola service, daily, 7 am—midnight, free (between Telluride and Mountain Village). Complimentary Dial-A-Ride and shuttle service in the Mountain Village.

DISTANCES IN MILES   Denver, CO 330; Durango, CO 125; Grand Junction, CO 127; Mesa Verde, CO 92; Montrose, CO 65; Phoenix, AZ 475.

Winter Park

Forget driving to Winter Park. Instead fly to Denver and ride the two-hour Ski Train, straight to the heart of the resort village. This memorable alternative runs twice weekly from Denver's Central Station (303-296-4754). Once you arrive, you'll be amazed at the array of amenities Winter Park provides. Boasting 130 trails serviced by 20 lifts, the biggest snowfall in Colorado, stunning vistas of the Continental Divide plus plenty of hotels, restaurants and après-ski activities, Winter Park has all the ingredients for a fun family getaway.

Advanced skiers head straight to Mary Jane base. Parking is free and basic amenities (including a ski school office) can be found inside the lodge. The lifts service numerous mogul runs, so suit up and hit the bumps. Families with kids in daycare or ski school should visit the main base, called the Village. The Children's Center (970-726-1551) is a brightly colored, fully stocked facility that keeps youngsters busy. Parents with children in daycare get a beeper for an extra $5 (reserve in advance). Just outside the

Village doors, a series of small hills and magic carpet serviced beginner terrain is perfect for first-timers.

Need a lesson? Try Winter Park's Family Private. The whole brood (up to six) can learn together for morning, afternoon or full-day lessons. All classes are guaranteed—if you don't feel that you've learned enough, you can keep trying until you catch on.

For kid-friendly fun, be sure to ski Discovery Park's simple slopes. Located just up from the Village, youngsters thrill to see the resort's mascot Willie the Moose playing around. Beginners can ride any chair on the mountain except Timberline, which takes you to Parsenn Bowl, an expert's paradise. Looking for a little untracked powder? Venture up to Vasquez Ridge. Superb views abound at all the peaks.

All accommodation, including on-slope condos at Zephyr Mountain Lodge, are reserved through the central reservation number (970-726-5587), or by visiting www.winterparkresort.com. Want evening entertainment? Try snowshoe-ing, a sleigh ride or hot air ballooning. Take a Snowcat tour and trek around the mountain in style. Call the Winter Park Tour Center for reservations (970-726-1616). Free shuttle service gets your family to and from on- and off-slope activities and accommodations.

WINTER PARK RESORT
CENTRAL LINE
970-726-5514
CENTRAL RESERVATION LINE
800-729-5813
SNOW REPORT
303-572-SNOW (7669)
ANNUAL SNOWFALL
365 inches.
INFORMATION
www.winterparkresort.com
SEASON
Mid-Nov—mid-April.
HOURS
Daily, 9 am—4 pm (opens at 8:30 am on weekends and holidays).

Also of interest at Winter Park is its National Sports Center for the Disabled. With the help of countless volunteers, you'll regularly see awe-inspiring skiers and riders overcoming their disabilities and carving up the slopes beside you. Other activities include snowboarding, snowshoeing, ski racing and cross-country skiing. Visit www.nscd.org or call (970-726-1540) for details.

👁 At a Glance

ADDRESS P.O. Box 36, Winter Park, CO 80482.

LOCATION North central Colorado.

TERRAIN MIX 3 mountains, 2,886 acres.

VERTICAL 3,060 feet (**PEAK** 12,060 feet. **BASE** 9,000 feet).

TRAILS 134 (9% Beginner, 21% Intermediate, 13% Advanced, 54% More Difficult, 3% Expert).

LIFTS 22 (8 high-speed quads, 4 triples, 7 doubles, 3 magic carpets).

DAILY LIFT TICKET RATES (US) Adults $54, seniors (62 to 69) $30, children (6 to 13) $18, over 69 and under 6 free.

SNOWMAKING 10%.

NIGHT SKIING None.

ACTIVITIES Moonlight snowmobiling, moonlight snowshoeing, Sun Spot Star Ride, Snowcat tours, indoor climbing wall, dog sledding, horse-drawn sleigh rides, hot air ballooning, Nordic skiing (970-726-1616).

BABYSITTERS Children's Center (970-726-1551) or Mountain Kids (970-726-8339).

DAYCARE Children's Center, daily, 8 am—4:30 pm (970-726-1551). Mountain Kids, day and evening childcare with activities (970-726-8339).

CHILDREN'S LESSONS AND CAMPS Children's Center (970-726-1551).

HOSPITAL 7 Mile Clinic (970-726-5514 ext. 1820). Granby Clinic (970-887-2117).

SPECIAL DEALS Discount tickets at over 400 outlets in Denver (King Soopers, Safeway, Albertson's, Breeze Rentals).

SPECIAL PROGRAMS National Sports Center for the Disabled (NSCD), $5 ridge rides with a snowmobile for expert skiers to access Vasquez Cirque, free beginner lessons (late Nov—mid-Dec), family private lessons (up to 6 family members), First Tracks.

GOOD MEETING PLACES The Lodge at Sunspot (on-slope), Coffee & Tea Market at Balcony House (Village).

DISTANCES IN MILES Boulder, CO 90; Denver, CO 67; Salt Lake City, UT 510.

NEW MEXICO

Taos Ski Valley

Tired of the mega-resort ski experience? Get back to basics at Taos Ski Valley, family-owned and operated since Ernie Blake built the resort 50 years ago. Located high in the Sangre de Cristo range at the southernmost outcropping of the Rockies, Taos has always been known for its challenging slopes and chutes, great sun, desert-dry powder and one of the top-rated ski schools in the nation. More recently, with the increase in local amenities and competitive pricing, industry publications have added accolades for both the resort's value and dining options.

In the past, skiing at Taos meant mingling with friendly locals in an environment free of lift lines and crowded slopes. The tradition remains unchanged today, particularly because Taos is one of only four skiers-only resorts left in North America. And it's also one of the only mountains where experts commonly go to learn new tricks. The late Blake believed that the exceptionally difficult terrain demanded exceptional instruction. That's why the ski school boasts a tradition of excellence in learning programs, and it doesn't hurt to have Olympic Gold Medallist Debbie Armstrong on staff either.

TAOS SKI VALLEY
CENTRAL LINE
505-776-2291
CENTRAL RESERVATION LINE
800-776-1111
or 505-776-2233
SNOW REPORT
505-776-2916
ANNUAL SNOWFALL
312 inches.
INFORMATION
www.skitaos.org
SEASON
Late Nov—early April.
HOURS
Daily, 9 am—4 pm.

At the base, children love the 18,000 square-foot creative learning center, Kinderkäfig (505-776-2291 ext. 1331), which comes complete with pint-sized tables, toilets and sinks. If you've got infants, BebeKare is licensed for tots aged six weeks to one year, with a ratio of one caregiver to two tots. The Kindercare program is for toddlers up to three years and boasts a one-to-three caregiver-to-child ratio. Potty-trained 3- to 12-year-olds can join the Junior Elite program, which includes lift ticket, rental and all-day lesson for $75 a day.

When you're ready to hit the slopes, don't be intimidated by the mile-long mogul run that looms dauntingly over the base. There are plenty of green runs that lead off every lift. But keep in mind the terrain is demanding. A blue trail at Taos might elsewhere be classified as black. For tots and new skiers, there are two magic carpets and a slow-speed double that services the gentle, beginner-only slopes near Kinderkäfig.

Off-slope adventures include exploring the Kit Carson National Forest on snowshoe or cross-country skis. Trade your poles for blades and join the kids for an afternoon of ice-skating or go snowmobiling. Drive 19 miles into the historic town of Taos, founded in the 17th century by Spanish soldiers. The town has a huge array of shops, museums and historic sites—including the fascinating 1,000-year-old Taos Pueblo and a spectacular side trip across the Rio Grande. Georgia O'Keefe helped popularize this authentic southwestern town. Art lovers have over 80 galleries to browse through.

From on-slope condos to simple A-frames, the mountain has numerous lodging possibilities. Call the Village of Taos Ski Valley Central Reservations (800-992-7669). Guests not used to the high altitude may want to acclimatize first in the town of Taos, since the base of the resort is over 9,000 feet. If your family does choose to stay slope-side, expect quiet nights except during major holidays, where magical torch-lit parades and fireworks spice up the evenings.

To save money, take advantage of the resort's $37 multi-day ticket rate, available daily (including holidays), but must be reserved in advance before December 1st. For air-and-lodging packages, including accommodations at Angel Fire Resort and direct charter service from Dallas International Airport, call (800-776-1111).

◉ At a Glance

ADDRESS   P.O. Box 90, Taos Ski Valley, NM 87525.
LOCATION   North central New Mexico.
TERRAIN MIX   2 mountains, 1,200 acres.
VERTICAL   3,274 feet (**PEAK** 12,481 feet. **BASE** 9,207 feet).
TRAILS   72 (24% Beginner, 25% Advanced, 51% Expert).
LIFTS   12 (4 quads, 1 triples, 5 doubles, 2 magic carpets).
DAILY LIFT TICKET RATES (US)   Adults $47, seniors (65 to 69) $32, youths (13 to 17) $37, children (0 to 12) $28, over 69 free.

SNOWMAKING 50% (100% of beginner and intermediate terrain).

NIGHT SKIING None.

ACTIVITIES Historic village, museums, art galleries, snowshoeing, Nordic skiing, tubing, ice-skating.

BABYSITTERS None.

DAYCARE Kiderkäfig, daily, 8 am—4:30 pm, 6 weeks to 3 years, reservations recommended (505-776-2291 ext. 1331).

CHILDREN'S LESSONS AND CAMPS Kinderkäfig (505-776-2291 ext. 1331).

HOSPITAL Mogul Medical Clinic (505-776-8421). Taos Hospital (505-758-8883).

SPECIAL DEALS Adult passes discounted if purchased before December 1st, Taos Card (discounts on lift tickets, lodging, meals and children's programs).

SPECIAL PROGRAMS Yellowbird first-timers ski school program (equipment rental and novice lift ticket for $55/day), Deb Armstrong clinics.

GOOD MEETING PLACES Tenderfoot Katies (base), Whistlestop (on-slope), Phoenix Restaurant (on-slope near Kachina back bowls).

DISTANCES IN MILES Albuquerque, NM 135; Dallas, TX 682; Denver, CO 300; Santa Fe, NM 72; Taos, NM 20.

CHAPTER FOUR

Western United States

Destination skiers and riders have a huge array of terrain possibilities along the western coast of the United States. Spread over four states—California, Nevada, Oregon and Washington—and two mountain ranges, families can pick and choose resorts in the location that suits them best.

California's Big Bear Lake area has long been a stomping ground for family day trippers from southern California. Further north, there's plenty of selection at Mammoth and its Woollywood ski school facilities for kids are top-notch.

The region's largest concentration of ski activity is based in Lake Tahoe. Expect excellent vacation packages, skiing and family programming. From the relatively small-sized Mt. Rose to the snowy slopes at Squaw Valley, everyone in your family will find terrain suited just for them. Plus, there are unlimited off-slope activities in this skier's Mecca. Diversions range from boating to casino gambling to hot air ballooning.

In Oregon, Mount Bachelor sits atop a volcanic cone and is usually open until mid-June. Families who want to ski a piece of history should plan to visit Timberline at Mt. Hood. With huge snowfalls and high alpine terrain, you can ski every month of the year at this resort. Looking for family-oriented skiing in Washington? Head to White Pass, located in the scenic Cascade Mountains.

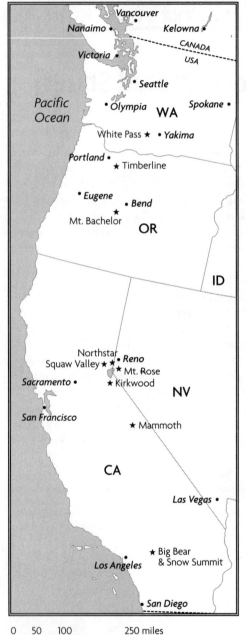

Western United States

Nevada
★ Mt. Rose

California
★ Big Bear &
  Snow Summit
★ Kirkwood
★ Mammoth
★ Northstar
★ Squaw Valley

Oregon
★ Mt. Bachelor
★ Timberline

Washington
★ White Pass

NEVADA

Mt. Rose

Location, location, location…never has an old adage been more true than when it is applied to a ski resort, and Mt. Rose-Ski Tahoe literally comes out on top!

Snowfall is key to all snow sports, and it doesn't get any better than at Mt. Rose. Sitting at 8,260 feet atop the eastern Sierra, this ski area has the highest base elevation of all Lake Tahoe resorts. So what does that mean? Great snow, a better quality base and superior springtime conditions.

The best way to experience it is to see for yourself. While there is no daycare, with Mt. Rose's even split among beginner, intermediate and expert terrain, there's plenty of opportunities to get your youngsters involved. If you need help getting started, call the Mt. Rose Ski School (775-849-0704 ext. 200). Beginners enjoy the terrain off Ponderosa, intermediates cruise Kit Carson bowl, while experts head for the peak and rip up the Northwest passage.

Looking for off-slope thrills? Mt. Rose's peak offers excellent views of Lake Tahoe and comes in tandem with the exciting nightlife of the "Biggest Little City." The resort's only 10 minutes from Incline Village and 25 miles from downtown Reno. So you can take your pick —enjoy the relaxed alpine environment of the lake or the high energy and value of Reno's 17,000 hotel rooms. Call Central Lodging (800-FOR-RENO) or (800-TAHOE-4-U) for more information.

Last, but by no means least, for those who don't like to waste valuable "on-snow" time battling traffic, the proximity of Mt.

MT. ROSE-SKI TAHOE

CENTRAL LINE
800-SKI-ROSE (754-7673) or 775-849-0704

CENTRAL RESERVATION LINE
800-FOR-RENO (367-7366) or 800-TAHOE4U (824-6348)

SNOW REPORT
877-687-6237

INFORMATION
www.skirose.com

ANNUAL SNOWFALL
400 inches.

SEASON
Mid-Nov—mid-April.

HOURS
Daily, 9 am—4 pm.

Rose-Ski Tahoe to the Reno/Tahoe International Airport is a huge bonus. Reno's "Gateway to the Sierras" is located only 22 miles (25 minutes drive time) from Reno/Tahoe International, and the mountain is the closest major ski resort to any international airport in the world.

👁 At a Glance

ADDRESS 22222 Mt. Rose Hwy., Reno, Nevada 89511.

LOCATION Western Nevada, Lake Tahoe area.

TERRAIN MIX 1 mountains, 1,000 acres.

VERTICAL 1,500 feet (**PEAK** 9,760 feet. **BASE** 8,260 feet).

TRAILS 43 (30% Beginner, 30% Advanced, 40% Expert).

LIFTS 12 (a six-pack, 2 quads, 2 triples, 1 magic carpet).

DAILY LIFT TICKETS RATES (US) Adults $45, youths (13 to 17) $35, children (6 to 12) $12, under 6 free.

SNOWMAKING 30%

NIGHT SKIING None.

ACTIVITIES Snowshoeing, Lake Tahoe and Reno nightlife.

BABYSITTERS None.

DAYCARE None.

CHILDREN'S LESSONS AND CAMPS Mt. Rose Ski School (775-849-0704 ext. 200).

HOSPITAL Washoe (775-982-4100).

SPECIAL DEALS Seniors (60 to 69) discounts and those over 70 ski free during mid-week, Tuesday special (2 for 1 full-day lift tickets), Wednesdays special (full-day lift ticket $19 for students with ID), Thursday special (full-day lift ticket $19 for women), Family Packages, Week day specials (anyone with a current season pass from another ski area gets full-day lift ticket for half price). All specials void during holiday season.

GOOD MEETING PLACES Zephyr Café (base of East Bowl), Higher Grounds (lobby of main lodge).

SPECIAL PROGRAMS Ski with Me (parents learn tips on instructing kids), Ladies Ski Esprit Thursdays (women's clinics), Silver Ski Fridays, USFS programs.

GETTING AROUND Mt. Rose Ski Shuttle, twice daily from several locations. Reservations are required (775-331-1147 or 800-822-6009).

DISTANCES IN MILES Las Vegas, NV 470; Reno, NV 22; Sacramento, CA 150; San Francisco, CA 240.

CALIFORNIA

Big Bear &
Snow Summit

First time visitors to the Los Angeles area are shocked to see snowcapped peaks north of the city. Despite their southern latitude, these mountains average six feet of snow each winter with elevations over 8,000 feet. Within a couple of hours, Los Angeles residents can drive to the resorts of Big Bear Lake and are guaranteed excellent snowmaking coverage and an array of enticing amenities. It's little wonder this area is a hit with families.

Two destination getaways are located side-by-side in the quaint resort town of Big Bear in the San Bernardino National Forest. So pack up the kids and make the trek. Both mountains feature innovative super pipes and terrain parks for the snowboarders in the family. Bear Mountain has an arsenal of hits and Snow Summit boasts a mile-long freestyle park with rail slides, hits, jumps and spines.

> **BEAR MOUNTAIN RESORT**
>
> **CENTRAL LINE**
> 909-585-2519
>
> **CENTRAL RESERVATION LINE**
> 800-4-BIG-BEAR (244-2327)
>
> **SNOW REPORT**
> 800-BEAR-MTN (232-7686)
>
> **ANNUAL SNOWFALL**
> 120 inches.
>
> **INFORMATION**
> www.bearmtn.com
>
> **SEASON**
> Nov—April.
>
> **HOURS**
> Daily, 8:30 am—4 pm (opens at 8 am and closes at 4:30 pm on weekends and holidays).

Big Bear Mountain is the only resort in the area to offer an adaptive ski program for disabled skiers. The ski school's Get Good Quick™ lessons offer special value rates that include equipment, one lesson and lift ticket for first- and second-time skiers and boarders. The lesson involves a unique coaching method using snow toys and Smart Terrain™. Snow Summit guarantees both private and group clinics—if you can't ski from the summit on your first day, you get free lessons until you can.

Big Bear is southern California's steepest and highest mountain and comes equipped with 100 percent snowmaking coverage. Both resorts are filled with excellent ski terrain, so plan to spend a few days in the nearby town of Big Bear Lake and test out both mountains. If you like peaceful, line-up-free skiing, try visiting during the week.

👁 At a Glance

BEAR MOUNTAIN RESORT

ADDRESS 43101 Goldmine Drive, Big Bear Lake, CA 92314.

LOCATION Southern California.

TERRAIN MIX 4 mountain peaks, 195 acres.

VERTICAL 1,665 feet (**PEAK** 8,805 feet. **BASE** 7,140 feet).

TRAILS 32 (25% Beginner, 50% Advanced, 25% Expert).

LIFTS 12 (3 high-speed quads, 2 triples, 4 doubles, 2 surface, 1 magic carpet).

DAILY LIFT TICKET RATES (US) Adults $35, children (6 to 12) $12, over 69 and under 6 free.

SNOWMAKING 100%

NIGHT SKIING None.

ACTIVITIES Tubing, United States Adaptive Recreation Center, Extreme test center (test out a variety of ski and snowboard equipment).

BABYSITTERS None.

DAYCARE None.

CHILDREN'S LESSONS AND CAMPS Magic Minor's Camp (909-585-2519).

HOSPITAL Big Bear Community Hospital (909-866-6501).

SPECIAL DEALS Kids (6 to 12) ski free Mon—Fri with paying adult. Offer void during holidays.

SPECIAL PROGRAMS Vertical Plus, Learn to Ski and Snowboard packages.

GOOD MEETING PLACES Trappers Restaurant (base), Silver Mountain Eatery (base).

DISTANCES IN MILES Los Angeles, CA 110; San Diego, CA 110.

SNOW SUMMIT MOUNTAIN RESORT

ADDRESS 880 Summit Blvd., P.O. Box 77, Big Bear Lake, CA 92315.

LOCATION Southern California.

TERRAIN MIX 2 mountains, 230 acres.

VERTICAL 1,200 feet (**PEAK** 8,200 feet. **BASE** 7,000 feet).

TRAILS 31 (10% Beginner, 65% Advanced, 25% Expert).

LIFTS 12 (2 high-speed quads, 2 quads, 2 triples, 5 doubles, 1 surface).

SNOW SUMMIT MOUNTAIN RESORT

CENTRAL LINE
909-866-5766

CENTRAL RESERVATION LINE
800-4-BIG-BEAR (244-2327)

SNOW REPORT
888-SUMMIT 1 (786648)

ANNUAL SNOWFALL
75 inches.

INFORMATION
www.snowsummit.com

SEASON
Mid-Nov—mid-April.

HOURS
Mon—Fri, 8 am—4:30 pm; Sat—Sun, 7:30 am—6 pm. Night skiing: Fri, Sat and holidays until 9 pm.

DAILY LIFT TICKET RATES (US) Adults $39, youths (13 to 19) $33, children (7 to 12) $12, under 7 free.
NIGHT LIFT TICKET RATES (US) Adults $31, children (7 to 12) $8, under 7 free.
SNOWMAKING 100%
NIGHT SKIING Weather dependant, on weekends and holidays only.
NIGHT PROGRAMS Night skiing and boarding on weekends and holidays.
ACTIVITIES Snowmobiling, snowshoeing.
BABYSITTERS None.
DAYCARE None.
CHILDREN'S LESSONS AND CAMPS Children's Ski & Snowboard School (909-866-5841).
HOSPITAL Big Bear Community Hospital (909-866-6501).
SPECIAL DEALS Snow Summit Guarantee, Half-Day Getaway Program, Ski or Ride Free on Your Birthday.
SPECIAL PROGRAMS GuaranSki learn-to-ski, Family Private.
GOOD MEETING PLACES Summit Haus (Mountain Express quad), Cafeteria at Bear Bottom Lodge
GETTING AROUND Dial-a-ride transport offered by MARTA (909-584-1111).
DISTANCES IN MILES Los Angeles, CA 110; Orange County, CA 90; San Diego, CA 130.

Kirkwood

When visiting Lake Tahoe, hop in the car for a beautiful 45-minute drive to Kirkwood. This resort has a family-sized vertical drop and a simple layout. The mountain is single faced, with a pedestrian village and secondary base set aside for beginners and the ski school.

When you arrive, head for the pedestrian area in front of the base lodge. It's the place to pick up lift tickets, sign up for lessons and have a cup of coffee before hitting the slopes. Non-skiers (two to six years) can spend their days in the Mini Mountain facility near Read Cliff's Day Lodge in Kirkwood's village. The daycare is not licensed for infants, however families can hire CPR certified babysitters to work day or night (ask at the lodge for a list of phone numbers). Tykes ages 4 to 12 can join the Mighty

KIRKWOOD MOUNTAIN RESORT

CENTRAL LINE
209-258-6000

CENTRAL RESERVATION LINE
800-967-7500

SNOW REPORT
209-258-3000

ANNUAL SNOWFALL
500 inches.

INFORMATION
www.kirkwood.com

SEASON
Mid-Nov—late April.

HOURS
Daily, 9 am—4 pm.

Mountain Children's Ski and Snowboard School. Drop-off is at the Timber Creek Base Lodge at the foot of the ski school slopes. Keep in mind that the daycare and school are separate.

Kirkwood's slopes get increasingly difficult as you move from right to left. Beginners stick to the Timber Creek area, while intermediates have the entire middle to themselves. Only advanced skiers should ride the Cornice lift to access black diamond terrain. Experts venture up to the steeps at Hully Gully and Thunder Saddle, or ride the uppermost chairs for challenging terrain. Before heading out, your children can pick up a copy of the Kid's Trail Map. It outlines secret, out-of-the-way spots they'll want to explore. Kirkwood also boasts over 50 miles of Nordic classic double track and skating trails. Cross-country tykes won't want to miss the Kiddie Kilometer—an interactive nature interpretive trail with life-sized animal cutouts along the way.

No matter where you ski, there are many places to eat. The Cornice Café (located at the car park) is a family favorite. Their specialized kids' menu comes with a choice of pasta, kid-sized burritos and chicken fingers and fries for under $5 each.

Outside the resort, Gold Country offers numerous options. Visit some of the oldest wineries in California, or go snowmobiling in the Sierra Nevada range. The nearby towns of Jackson and Sutter Creek offer an eclectic mix of shopping and dining. You can drive to Tahoe and see the sights or hit the casinos for an evening.

With the recent addition of brand new condos and a full-service hotel, Kirkwood is becoming a skiers' community. Real estate is booming in the area, and more families are starting to make their way from the coast to this Gold Country gem.

👁 At a Glance

ADDRESS P.O. Box 1, Kirkwood, CA 95646.
LOCATION Northeastern California.
TERRAIN MIX 3 peaks, 2,300 acres.
VERTICAL 2,000 feet (**PEAK** 9,800 feet. **BASE** 7,800 feet).
TRAILS 65 (15% Beginner, 50 % Intermediate, 20% Advanced, 15% Expert).
LIFTS 12 (2 quads, 7 triples, 1 double, 2 surface).
DAILY LIFT TICKET RATES (US) Adults $49, seniors (65 to 69) $25, youths (13 to 22) $29, seniors over 70 and children (6 to 12) $10, under 6 free.
SNOWMAKING 8%.
NIGHT SKIING None.

ACTIVITIES Sleigh rides, kids' après-ski in Mountain Village on Saturdays and holidays, Nordic skiing, ice-skating, snowshoeing, sleigh rides, Family Fun Zone (tubing, sledding, and rides on the Snow Volcano), dog sledding, Spa and Massage Center, snowmobiling, ice fishing, hot springs.

BABYSITTERS Contact (209-258-7293) or Mini Mountain Childcare (209-258-7274).

DAYCARE Mini Mountain Child Care Center, 2 to 6 years (209-258-7274).

CHILDREN'S LESSONS AND CAMPS Mighty Mountain Children's Ski & Snowboard School (209-258-7754).

HOSPITAL Barton Memorial Hospital (530-541-3420).

SPECIAL DEALS Ski Free (lodging and ski free program from Sun to Thu).

SPECIAL PROGRAMS All Mountain Day Camps, Ladies All Conditions camps, North American Ski Training Center, Multi Day Performance Ski School for Advanced Skiers with Backcountry and Avalanche Awareness.

GOOD MEETING PLACES Mountain Village Plaza (base), Timber Creek Day Lodge Cafeteria (Ski School base).

DISTANCES IN MILES Reno, NV 82; Sacramento, CA 100; San Francisco, CA 178; Tahoe City, CA 58.

Mammoth

Seeking alpine scenery just hours from Los Angeles and San Francisco? No need to look farther than Mammoth—southern California's major-mountain resort located high in the Sierra Nevada range. This vacation spot caters to families by offering affordable prices, spacious, kid-friendly accommodations and entertainment galore.

If your kids need ski lessons, this is the place to take them. At the Mammoth Mountain Sports School, choose between two excellent learning centers. In the Main Lodge, custom-designed Wollywood comes equipped with pint-sized seats, a play area and tree house. At Canyon Lodge, there's an equally entertaining 4,000 square-foot center called Canyon Kids. Both locations offer

---

MAMMOTH MOUNTAIN

CENTRAL LINE
760-934-0745

CENTRAL RESERVATION LINE
1-800-MAMMOTH
(626-6684)

SNOW REPORT
888-SNOWRPT
(766-9778)

ANNUAL SNOWFALL
385 inches.

INFORMATION
www.Mammoth
Mountain.com

SEASON
Mid-Nov—mid-June.

HOURS
Daily, 8:30 am—4 pm.

full-day programs. For $99 each child gets lunch, a lift ticket, equipment rental and five hours of instruction.

Are your tots too young for skis? They can spend the day at Small World Day Care (760-934-0646) located at the Mammoth Mountain Inn across from the Main Lodge. Park in the drop-off parking zone and take your kids inside to the bright, age-related rooms. Don't worry about leaving infants. The daycare is licensed for children of all ages.

Now you're ready to start off at the beginner terrain, which is accessed by magic carpet or high-speed quad near either the Main or Canyon Lodge. As your confidence increases, head to the Broadway and Stump Alley Express quads for some interme-diate action. While only advanced and expert skiers can carve up the summit terrain, anyone can ride the gondola and enjoy the view at the Panorama Lookout. Snowboarders face challenges surfing the resort's three terrain parks and three half pipes.

For après-ski or off-slope action, make tracks to the Tamarack Cross-Country Ski Center. Here you'll discover 28 miles of trails that meander through Inyo National Forest. Or, visit the tubing center near the Mill Café base. For added fun, hop aboard a hot air balloon or spend the evening visiting the town of Mammoth, which boasts a full range of services from restaurants to shopping to movies. Teens will want to hang out at the arcade on Old Mammoth Road. No need to drive. Six free bus lines service the town and resort.

Things keep changing at Mammoth. Canadian developer Intrawest plans to add another condo village. Each unit will offer functional facilities in deluxe surroundings. In the next few years, this major expansion combined with rustic dining and shopping facilities will be a welcome addition to this progressive commu-nity.

◉ At a Glance

ADDRESS Box 24, Mammoth Lakes, CA 93546.
LOCATION Central California.
TERRAIN MIX 1 mountain, 3,500 acres.
VERTICAL 3,100 feet (**PEAK** 11,053 feet. **BASE** 7,953 feet).
TRAILS 150 (30% Beginner, 40% Advanced, 30% Expert).
LIFTS 30 (2 gondolas, 1 six-pack, 8 high-speed quads, 1 quad, 8 triples, 6 doubles, 2 surface, 2 magic carpets).

DAILY LIFT TICKET RATES (US)   Adults $56, youths (13 to 18) $42, seniors (65 to 79) and children (7 to 12) $28, over 80 and under 7 free.
SNOWMAKING   25%.
NIGHT SKIING   None.
ACTIVITIES   Cross-country, snowmobiling (kid sizes available), snowshoeing, sleigh rides, ice-skating, dog sledding.
BABYSITTERS   Small World Childcare (760-934-0646).
DAYCARE   Small World Childcare, daily, 8 am — 4:30 pm, newborns to 12 years (760-934-0646).
CHILDREN'S LESSONS AND CAMPS   Mammoth Kids Sport School (760-934-0685).
HOSPITAL   Mammoth Hospital (760-934-3311).
SPECIAL DEALS   Visit www.mammothmountain.com for seasonal specials.
SPECIAL PROGRAMS   Woman's Ski Seminar, Adaptive lessons, Unbound Park sessions, AJ Kitt Ski Racing School, Mammoth Masters Team, Forest Service Tours.
GOOD MEETING PLACES   Mid Chalet (base of Panorama gondola), Cornice Café (Main Lodge).
GETTING AROUND   Mammoth California Transit, daily, 7 am — 5:30 pm (to and from several points in the village). Night service available on Fri, Sat, and holidays until 11 pm.
DISTANCES IN MILES   Los Angeles, CA 307; Reno, NV 168; San Francisco, CA 320.

Northstar

According to a recent poll in *Ski Magazine*, Northstar serves up California's best family programs. With great value vacation packages in an unbeatable locale — Lake Tahoe — this resort has it all, from ski and snowboard lessons to daycare, riding stables and a cross-country ski center.

When you arrive, unload your gear at the 15-minute drop-off parking zone, or find a spot in the lot and ride the shuttle bus to the pedestrian village. If you'd rather park out front, be prepare to spend $14 a day. Once you've left the wheels behind, head to the Minors' Camp daycare center

NORTHSTAR-AT-TAHOE

CENTRAL LINE
530-562-1010

CENTRAL RESERVATION LINE
800-GO-NORTH (466-6784)

SNOW REPORT
530-562-1330

ANNUAL SNOWFALL
350 inches.

INFORMATION
www.skinorthstar.com

SEASON
Late Nov — mid-April.

HOURS
Daily, 8:30 am — 4 pm (until 9 pm weekends and holidays).

(530-562-2278) located above the main ticketing office. The center caters to kids from two to ten years old (must be potty trained) and distributes pagers to parents. The daycare has a Kids' Happy Hour from 4:30 pm to 6:30 pm on Saturdays and holidays.

Have tots who need lessons? Northstar's Star Kids ski and snowboard program operates a 5,000 square-foot, mid-mountain facility that also offers rentals. If you'd like to improve your technique, visit the Snowsports Learning Center (530-562-1010). Group lessons begin at 10 am and noon with private lessons running all day. Northstar offers free Vertical Improvement lessons for advanced and expert skiers on a first-come, first-served basis. Lessons begin at the top of Mount Pluto every hour between 10 am and 2 pm.

If you want to ski as a family and are looking for some tips to help your tykes learn faster—check out the Mommy, Daddy and Me clinics. They are offered Sunday through Friday at 2:30 pm at the children's Snowsports Learning Center, adjacent to the Lodge at Big Springs. Northstar has also created the interchangeable Parent Predicament lift ticket. For $52, parents can share a day pass and bring their gear to the Parent Zone, located at the mid-station base. It's a cozy family area with tables and chairs for lunch and lots of toys for kids.

Pick up a map before you hit the slopes. Snowboarders should visit the resort's terrain parks, especially the popular Snowbomb.com. This park is located at Ground Zero and features a half pipe and a new super pipe that's almost a mile long. Paw Parks are the rage for kids. These little hideaways in the woods combines miniature terrain features and snow play areas. Experts should bring their cameras up to the black diamond East Ridge Trail. Intermediates have plenty of groomed runs to coast down—Northstar regularly re-grooms a couple of trails around noon.

For evening excitement, visit the Polaris Park family recreation area at the top of the gondola. Here you can tube, use snow toys, ski or board. Hungry after a long day on the slopes? Try one of the resort's two family-style restaurants—Timbercreek or Pedro's. Or you can use the Pizza Phone while you're at Polaris Park and when you reach the base, your order will be ready.

With accolades from many ski and family publications, Northstar is a haven for ski families. It combines moderate terrain, great programs and sensible pricing, which is a boon to families with young children.

👁 At a Glance

ADDRESS P.O. Box 129, Truckee, CA 96160.
LOCATION Northeastern California.
TERRAIN MIX 1 mountain, 2,420 acres.
VERTICAL 2,280 feet (**PEAK** 8,610 feet. **BASE** 6,330 feet).
TRAILS 70 (25% Beginner, 50% Advanced, 25% Expert).
LIFTS 15 (a 6-person gondola, 5 high-speed quads, 2 triples, 2 doubles, 3 surface, 2 magic carpets).
DAILY LIFT TICKET RATES (US) Adults $52, seniors (60 to 69) $28, seniors (over 70) $5, youths (13 to 22) $42, children (5 to 12) $15, under 5 free.
SNOWMAKING 50%.
NIGHT SKIING Polaris Park, 2 lifts serving beginner terrain.
ACTIVITIES Polaris Park (night skiing, snowboarding, tubing and snow toys), Swim and Racquet Club, snowshoeing, Nordic skiing, sleigh rides, dog sledding, snowmobiling.
BABYSITTERS Contact Minors' Camp (530-562-2278).
DAYCARE Minors' Camp, daily, 8:30 am—4:30 pm, 2 to 6 years (530-562-2278).
CHILDREN'S LESSONS AND CAMPS Snowsports Learning Center (530-562-2471).
HOSPITAL Tahoe Forest Hospital (530-587-6011).
SPECIAL DEALS Lodge and Learn free packages, Afternoon Credit (turn in your day pass by 12:30 pm and receive credit for your next visit).
SPECIAL PROGRAMS Lunchtime Grooming, Vertical Plus, Starkids and Shredkids (skiing, tubing, lunch, lesson and rentals) Paw Parks.
GOOD MEETING PLACES Parent Zone at Big Springs (mid-mountain), Pedro's (base).
GETTING AROUND Free shuttle from Truckee Tahoe Airport or Amtrak and Greyhound depots in Truckee, free on-site shuttle.
DISTANCES IN MILES Reno, NV 40; Sacramento, CA 96; San Francisco, CA 196; Truckee, CA 6.

Squaw Valley

Five miles north of Lake Tahoe on the Truckee River, Squaw Valley is a fabulous winter playground for families. It started out as a local's hill in 1949 and grew to host the Winter Olympics in 1960. Now considered one of the largest resorts in North

America, Squaw Valley offers over 4,000 acres of ski terrain and boasts one of the most advanced lift systems on the continent. This well-known skier and rider mammoth comes complete with velvety slopes, incredible steeps and (important for families) a large facility for kids.

Located at the base, the state-licensed Children's World is a 12,000 square-foot space designed especially for the younger set (ages 2 to 12). Here you'll find the Children's World Ski School, which offers age-specific packages for skiing and snowboarding, including meals, rentals, lift tickets and lessons. Toddler Care (530-581-7166), for two- to three-year-olds, provides tykes with fun things to do, such as arts and crafts, snow play and story time. Reservations are recommended.

If your family skis together, Squaw Valley has myriad possibilities and a view of the Sierra Nevada that can't be beat. The mountain is shaped mostly by bowls, so intermediates and experts get to ski excellent, western-style terrain. Snowboarders test out the half pipes or spend the afternoon at the terrain parks. For beginners, the resort's easiest slopes are located at the top of the mountain so everyone gets a chance to experience that top-of-the-world feeling. Ride the Cable Car up to High Camp (elevation 8,200 feet) where five lifts service plenty of gently rolling terrain.

When your brood needs a break, stop at High Camp, the center of the resort's upper mountain. Go for a skate at the Olympic Ice Pavilion, throttle down the tube park, or stroll through the Olympic Winter Games Museum. There are three restaurants in case anyone is hungry. Do you like spring skiing? Visit Squaw Valley after mid-March and pack your bathing suit for a dip at the High Camp Swimming Lagoon and Spa.

After your skis are packed away, keep active at the indoor rock climbing facility, or enjoy snowshoeing, sleigh rides, dog sledding or relaxing at the spa. Spend the evening in Tahoe City and experience a world-class tourist town, complete with all the amenities from shopping to movie theatres to restaurants. If you can't get enough carving, try the resort's 3.6 miles of night skiing. Your day lift ticket works at night too.

SQUAW VALLEY

CENTRAL LINE
530-583-6985

CENTRAL RESERVATION LINE
800-545-4350

SNOW REPORT
530-583-6955

ANNUAL SNOWFALL
450 inches

INFORMATION
www.squaw.com

SEASON
Mid-Nov—mid-May.

HOURS
Daily, 9 am—4pm (opens at 8:30 on weekends). Night Skiing: 4 pm—9 pm.

There are many accommodation options in Squaw Valley, including full-service hotels and a luxury resort. Call 1–888-SNOW-3-2-1 or 800-545-4350 for details. With a $250 million investment by mega-resort developer Intrawest, expect improved slope-side accommodations and shopping in the new village at Squaw Valley in the near future.

◉ At a Glance

ADDRESS   1960 Squaw Valley Road, Box 2007, Olympic Valley, CA 96146.

LOCATION   Northeastern California.

TERRAIN MIX   6 mountains, 4,000 acres.

VERTICAL   2,850 feet (**PEAK** 9,050 feet. **BASE** 6,200 feet).

TRAILS   100, plus open bowls (25% Beginner, 45% Intermediate, 30% Expert).

LIFTS   30 (1 cable car, 1 gondola, a 6-person pulse, 3 high-speed six-packs, 4 high-speed quads, 1 quad, 8 triples, 7 doubles, 3 surface, 1 magic carpet).

DAILY LIFT TICKET RATES (US)   Adults $56, seniors (65 to 75) and youths (13 to 15) $28, under 13 $5, over 75 free.

NIGHT LIFT TICKET RATES (US)   Adults $20, seniors (65 to 75) and youths (13 to 15) $10, under 13 $5, over 75 free.

SNOWMAKING   10%.

NIGHT SKIING   Cable Car and Riviera Lift, 2000 vertical feet, 400 acres.

ACTIVITIES   Night-lit half pipe, swimming, indoor climbing wall, tubing, Adventure Ropes course, scenic Cable Car rides, Nordic skiing, Spa & Fitness center, snowshoeing, dog sledding, sleigh rides, arcade games.

BABYSITTERS   Contact Children's World (530-581-7225).

DAYCARE   Children's World, daily, 8:30 am — 4 pm, 2 to 3 years (530-581-7225).

CHILDREN'S LESSONS AND CAMPS   Children's World (530-581-7225).

HOSPITAL   Tahoe Forest Hospital (530-587-6011).

SPECIAL DEALS   Free night skiing with day pass, Frequent Ski & Board program (ski 4 days and the 5th is free), check for other deals at www.squawvacations.com

SPECIAL PROGRAMS   Adaptive Ski School (530-581-7263).

GOOD MEETING PLACES   Fireplace at Dave's Deli (base), Crossroads Café (mid-mountain).

DISTANCES IN MILES   Reno, NV 42; Sacramento, CA 96; San Francisco, CA 196.

OREGON

Mt. Bachelor

Families from Oregon, Washington and Northern California are drawn to Mt. Bachelor for its great vistas, superb network of high-speed lifts and lengthy season. The mountain's classic volcanic shape means lots of variety in terrain. With plenty of dry snow and a history of family-friendly skiing, it's an excellent winter vacation spot.

On-slope, there are six day lodges for all your skiing needs. Two of these, Sunrise and West Village, offer amenities including daycare. If your family is laden with beginners, make Sunrise your home base. While it only has space for ten kids in its daycare, Mt. Bachelor's easiest slopes are right outside the door. Or try West Village, which is more crowded, but has a larger daycare (capacity 60).

Mt. Bachelor offers many ski and ride programs, private and group lessons for half or full days. There's even a Guaranteed Kids program! For $60 a day, children aged 7 to 12 years receive a lift ticket, lunch and instruction in a dynamic program that promises to keep teaching as long as it takes to learn the basics.

Ready to hit the slopes? Over 55 percent of the resort's terrain caters to advanced and expert skiers, while the remaining slopes are perfect for beginners and intermediates. For superb open bowl skiing, ride the Summit Express. Snowboarders have access to the entire mountain, but many like to spend time catching air at the mountain's half pipe, triple jump and terrain park. Looking for a mid-mountain break? Try the Pine Marten Lodge for unparalleled vistas of the Cascade Range and delicious treats.

MT. BACHELOR

CENTRAL LINE
800-829-2442 or
541-382-2607

CENTRAL RESERVATION LINE
800-829-2442

SNOW REPORT
541-382-7888

ANNUAL SNOWFALL
350 inches.

INFORMATION
www.mtbachelor.com

SEASON
Mid-Nov—June.

HOURS
Daily, 9 am—4 pm
(opens at 8 am on
weekends and
holidays).

Munch Tuscan-style food at Scapolo's, smoothies at Pinnacles or gourmet fare at the Skier's Palate.

Keep in mind that Mt. Bachelor offers no on-slope lodging. Guests stay in Bend where facilities tend to be cheapest, or overnight at one of the many upscale condos in Sunriver. Both towns have après-ski entertainment including cinemas, shopping malls and restaurants. For some kid-specific fun, head to the nearby town of Redmond and visit the Kidzone and Crazy Mama's Pizzeria complete with a huge, three-level soft play area, billiards tables and video games.

In the next few years, look for big changes at this northwestern classic. Powdr Corporation (owners of Alpine Meadows, CA and Park City, UT) recently bought Mt. Bachelor. Visit www.mtbachelor.com for updates on the resort's development schedule.

👁 At a Glance

ADDRESS P.O. Box 1031, Bend, OR 97709.

LOCATION Central Oregon.

TERRAIN MIX 2 mountain faces, 3,683 acres.

VERTICAL 3,365 feet (**PEAK** 9,065 feet. **BASE** 6,300 feet).

TRAILS 71 (15% Beginner, 25% Intermediate, 35% Advanced, 25% Expert).

LIFTS 12 (7 high-speed quads, 3 triples, 2 surface).

DAILY LIFT TICKET RATES (US) Adults $43, Seniors (over 64), youths (13 to 18) and students with ID $32, children (7 to 12) $22, under 7 ski free.

SNOWMAKING None.

NIGHT SKIING None.

ACTIVITIES Nordic skiing, dog sledding, snowshoeing, sleigh rides, snowmobiling (at local snow parks).

BABYSITTERS None.

DAYCARE Mt. Bachelor Daycare, daily, 8:30 am—4 pm (opens at 7:30 am on weekends), 6 weeks to 10 years (800-829-2442).

CHILDREN'S LESSONS AND CAMPS Mountain Masters (4 to 12) (800-829-2442), Mighty Mites, Mountaineers, High Cascade Snowboard Camps (800-334-4272).

HOSPITAL St. Charles Medical Center (541-382-4321).

SPECIAL DEALS Express Pass (entitles you to lift ticket discounts), family 4-pack season pass.

SPECIAL PROGRAMS Forest Service tours, Adaptive Ski Program, Guaranteed Learn to Ski/Board lessons, interpretive snowshoe walks, ride along with a pro-Patroller, Mt. Bachelor Ski Education Foundation (541-333-0002).

GOOD MEETING PLACES Pine Marten Lodge (mid-mountain), Sunrise Lodge (base).

GETTING AROUND   Mt. Bachelor Super Shuttle, 7 am — 4:30 pm, $4 round-trip from Bend or $5 from Sunriver.

DISTANCES IN MILES   Bend, OR 22; Eugene, OR 150; Portland, OR 450; Seattle, WA 630.

Timberline

A**S** one of the most famous ski lodges in North America, Timberline Lodge is a popular place for skiing families. Situated within an hour's drive of Portland International Airport, this resort is one of Oregon's most-visited tourist attractions. The slope-side historic hotel offers superb accommodation with plenty of extras for kids, such as a games and movie room.

Despite Timberline's fame, its location 6,000 feet up the side of Mt. Hood limits the amount of daily traffic, so families enjoy skiing together without the hassle of long lift lines. Just arriving? Start your day off at the Wy'east Day Lodge, which houses two restaurants, rental, repair and retail shops and the ski patrol headquarters. Although there is no daycare service offered at the resort, the Ski School takes skiers as young as four and boarders as young as six.

For a shot at Timberline's intermediate terrain, hop on any of the three chairs. Try cruising off the Magic Mile quad. Beginners love to learn on Conway's Corner and the Lower runs. You'll need to be an expert to attain the highest vertical in the Pacific Northwest. Timberline's high-speed Palmer Express quad takes you to the top, where there's steep and bowl carving to enjoy. Snowboarding? Head to the terrain park adjacent to the Stormin' Norman chair.

TIMBERLINE AT MT. HOOD

CENTRAL LINE
503-622-7979

CENTRAL RESERVATION LINE
800-547-1406
or 503-231-5400

SNOW REPORT
503-222-2211

ANNUAL SNOWFALL
550 inches.

INFORMATION
www.timberlinelodge.com

SEASON
Year-round (short closure in September for maintenance).

HOURS
Daily, 9 am — 4 pm (until 10 pm on Fri and Sat during the winter).

Can't get enough skiing during the day? Try carving up the slopes on Friday and Saturday nights. Due to the massive snow-fall, Timberline has recently become a year-round ski destination. Now you can work your edges in the summer along side the US National team on the runs off Palmer quad. If you're flying and want to avoid driving the windy road to the resort, call Timberline Airport Transfers at (503-668-7433).

👁 At a Glance

ADDRESS Timberline, Timberline Lodge, OR 97028.
LOCATION North central Oregon.
TERRAIN MIX 1 mountain, 1,430 acres.
VERTICAL 3,590 feet (**PEAK** 8,540 feet. **BASE** 4,950 feet).
TRAILS 32 (30% Beginner, 50% Advanced, 20% Expert).
LIFTS 7 (4 high-speed quads, 1 triple, 1 double, 1 magic carpet).
DAILY LIFT TICKET RATES (US) Adults $37, children (7 to 12) $21, under 7 free.
NIGHT TICKET RATES (US) Adults $18, children (7 to 12) $15, under 7 free.
SNOWMAKING None.
NIGHT SKIING 3 lifts, 11 runs.
NIGHT PROGRAMS Family movies in Barlow Room, shuffleboard, ping pong and board games, sauna, spa, outdoor swimming pool, movie room, museum, US Forest Service tours, Historic Lodge, Brewery tours.
BABYSITTERS Inquire at Timberline Lodge (503-622-7979).
DAYCARE None.
CHILDREN'S LESSONS AND CAMPS Bruno's Children's Learning Center (503-231-5402).
HOSPITAL Mt. Hood Medical Center (503-674-1122).
SPECIAL DEALS Check www.timberlinelodge.com for seasonal specials.
SPECIAL PROGRAMS Hotel guests get reduced price kids' menu and free for those under 8.
GOOD MEETING PLACES Timberline Lodge (main foyer), Wy'east Day Lodge.
DISTANCES IN MILES Portland, OR 55; Seattle, WA 180.

WASHINGTON

White Pass

Where can you access 32 runs in less than five minutes? At White Pass' high-speed detachable quad, the Great White Express. And that's not all. Only 12 miles from Mt. Rainer in the breathtaking Cascade Mountain range, White Pass has abundant snowfall, wide variety of terrain, an innovative ski school program and friendly hospitality.

Sixty percent of the resort's terrain is rated intermediate, with the remainder split between expert and beginner—the perfect mix for families. Have pint-sized snowboarders? Visit the mountain's half pipe, quarter pipes and big air kickers. If your tykes (ages two to six) are too young to be on the slopes, drop them off at White Pass' cozy daycare center. On weekends and holidays, the daycare offers as Peewee Skee program where kids get special hour of sliding out on the slopes (509-672-3106).

WHITE PASS SKI AREA
CENTRAL LINE
509-672-3101
CENTRAL RESERVATION LINE
509-672-3131
SNOW REPORT
579-672-3100
ANNUAL SNOWFALL
350 inches.
INFORMATION
www.skiwhitepass.com
SEASON
Mid-Nov—early May.
HOURS
Daily, 8:45 am—4 pm (until 10 pm Fri, Sat and holidays).

Other popular programs include the full-day Kids' Clinic Weekends, which include supervised lunch and instruction offered on alternating weekends from January to March. Older children and adults can join the Guaranteed to Ski the Mountain program, which combines superior shaped skis and tailored instruction to get you down any slope. Call the Learning Center for details (509-672-3100).

For the energetic, try night skiing on Fridays and Saturdays, or head to the resort's Nordic skating lane and scenic cross-country ski trails that encircle a picturesque lake and climb into the Wenatchee National Forest. White Pass offers several mid-week ski and stay value packages at local hotels and motels. Stay slopeside at the Village Inn (509-672-3131).

No matter where you stay. You can wake up to un-crowded slopes and an at-home feeling. Families should take advantage of this relatively undiscovered Cascade hideaway.

◉ At a Glance

ADDRESS P.O. Box 3030, White Pass, WA 98937.

LOCATION Central Washington Cascades.

TERRAIN MIX 1 mountain, 635 acres.

VERTICAL 1,500 feet (**PEAK** 6,000 feet. **BASE** 4,500 feet).

TRAILS 32 (20% Beginner, 60% Advanced, 20% Expert).

LIFTS 6 (1 high-speed quad, 1 triple, 2 doubles, 1 surface, 1 magic carpet).

DAILY LIFT TICKET RATES (US) Adults $34, seniors (65 to 72) $22, over 72 and under 7 free.

NIGHT LIFT TICKET RATES IN (US) Adults $15, seniors (65 to 72) and children (7 to 12) $12, over 72 and under 7 free.

SNOWMAKING 6%.

NIGHT SKIING Triple chair serving 120 acres.

ACTIVITIES Glow Nights Lesson Series, cross-country skiing, ice-skating, snowshoeing.

BABYSITTERS Contact Daycare (509-672-3106).

DAYCARE Daycare at White Pass, daily, 8:30 am—4:30 pm, 2 to 6 years (509-672-3106).

CHILDREN'S LESSONS AND CAMPS The Learning Center (509-672-3101).

HOSPITAL Yakima Memorial Hospital (509-575-8000).

SPECIAL DEALS Night skiing free with purchase of daily lift ticket, Vertical Advantage.

GOOD MEETING PLACES Ticket booth (base), bottom of chair 4 (on-slope)

SPECIAL PROGRAMS Women's Only Workshop, Prime Timer's Workshop, Guaranteed to Ski the Mountain program.

DISTANCES IN MILES Portland, OR 175; Seattle, WA 150; Tacoma, WA 111.

CHAPTER FIVE

Eastern Canada

La belle province, Québec, offers a unique skiing experience in North America; continental atmosphere without the transatlantic flight. Montréal is the perfect base from which to start your skiing vacation. With a centrally located train station and airport, the resorts listed in this chapter are only a short car ride from the vibrant, bilingual city.

Due north in the Laurentians, families will find the quaint Mont Habitant and lively Mont Blanc within an hour and a half drive. The tremendously popular mega-resort, Mont Tremblant, is a bit farther along Highway 15. Here you'll find plenty of shopping and activities for the non-skiers in your family, as well as exceptional skiing facilities.

Owl's Head, a family-run resort, lies an hour and a half south-east of the metropolis in the Cantons de l'est (Eastern Townships), near the Vermont border. To see one of the only remaining walled cities, buckle up and head to Québec City. Here, Mont-Sainte-Anne's superb slopes serve up excellent skiing, a top-rated ski school and an Enchanted Forest just for kids. If you visit in late January, take part in the annual winter festival, Carnaval (www.carnaval.qc.ca).

Don't be deterred if you can't speak French. Almost everyone is bilingual. Also, be prepared to eat well. French Canadian cuisine is some of the best (and least costly) on the continent. The best part? Paying Canadian prices makes skiing in Québec an affordable alternative to resorts across the border. For best flight schedules and competitive prices call Air Canada (888-247-2262) or visit their web site at www.aircanada.ca. Air Canada and its regional partners offer more non-stop flights to Canadian cities than all other carriers combined.

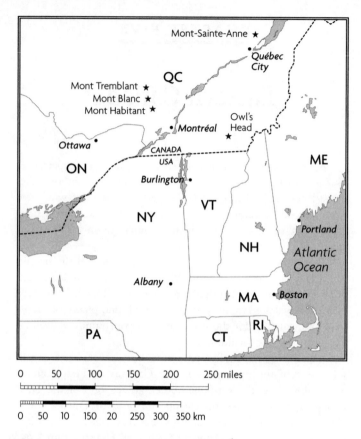

0   50   100   150   200   250 miles

0   50   10   150   20   250   300   350 km

Eastern Canada

Laurentians
★ Mont Habitant
★ Mont Blanc
★ Mont Tremblant

Eastern Townships
★ Owl's Head

Québec City
★ Mont-Saint-Anne

LAURENTIANS

Mont Habitant

Looking for a family-oriented mountain with plenty of deals and personal service, that is small enough for your kids to feel comfortable heading off on their own? Then plan a trip to Mont Habitant, located 45 minutes from Montréal in the Laurentian Mountains.

With only three lifts and eight runs, Mont Habitant is definitely the place to bring beginners. The resort's ski school offers a variety of lesson packages from private to small groups, plus Christmas and school holiday multi-day camp specials. The mountain's 100 percent snowmaking coverage means there is always good snow for skiers. Boarders have their own nook at the terrain park.

Each day of the week, Mont Habitant offers something special. On Mondays, guests get a free pasta dish with the purchase of a regular lift ticket. Free fondue is available on Tuesday, Wednesday and Thursday nights. Also on Thursdays, moms pay $10 for lift tickets and daycare is free. If you're flying in from out of town, National Car Rental offers free day passes with certain car rentals (800-227-7368).

Overnighters should check out the ski-in Auberge Mont Habitant (450-227-2637). Each room comes with a small kitchenette, sleeps four, and kids under 12 stay free. There are lots of things to do, too—Mont Habitant offers ice-skating and night skiing. Investigate a variety of après- and non-ski options in the local tourist town, St. Sauveur des Monts, which has dining, sleigh rides and shopping opportunities.

MONT HABITANT

CENTRAL LINE
450-227-2637
or 514-393-1821

CENTRAL LODGING
450-227-2637

SNOW REPORT
450-227-2637

ANNUAL SNOWFALL
120 inches.

INFORMATION
www.monthabitant.com

SEASON
Mid-Nov—mid-April.

HOURS
Daily, 9 am—10 pm (until 10:30 pm on Fri, opens at 8:30 am on weekends)

Mont Habitant has teamed up with Mont Blanc and Grey Rocks to form the Laurentian Tri Area. Lift tickets are transferable, so buy a weeklong ski pass at Mont Habitant and when you're ready for something different, head to one of the other mountains. This three-in-one deal is a hit with vacationing families.

👁 At a Glance

ADDRESS 12, boulevard des Skieurs, Saint-Sauveur-des-Monts, Québec J0R 1R2.

LOCATION Central Québec.

TERRAIN MIX 1 mountain, 55 acres.

VERTICAL 551 feet (**PEAK** 1,300 feet. **BASE** 600 feet).

TRAILS 11 (30% Beginner, 40% Advanced, 30% Expert).

LIFTS 3 (1 quad, 1 double, 1 surface).

DAILY LIFT TICKET RATES (CDN) Adults $31, seniors (60 to 69) and youths (13 to 20) $27, children (6 to 12) $20, seniors (over 69) and tots (under 6) $6.

NIGHT LIFT TICKET RATES (CDN) Adults $22, seniors (60 to 69) and youths (13 to 20) $18, children (6 to 12) $16, seniors (over 69) and tots (under 6) $6.

SNOWMAKING 100%.

NIGHT SKIING 3 lifts, 55 acres.

ACTIVITIES Ice-skating.

BABYSITTERS None.

DAYCARE Le Petit Soleil, 9 am—5 pm, 2 to 5 years (450-227-2637).

CHILDREN'S LESSONS AND CAMPS Ski & Snowboard School (450-227-2637), Club ADO (4-hour session for teens includes evaluation, moguls, videos, snowboard).

HOSPITAL Centre Hospitalier Laurentien (816-324-4000).

SPECIAL DEALS 10-Ticket Booklet, Option Passes (20 % off lift ticket on weekends), Ultimate Season Pass (ski free at Gray Rocks and Mont Blanc).

SPECIAL PROGRAMS Adult Competition races, Family Program (family lessons on Sun), Pro-Vedette (55+ ski together on Wed).

GOOD MEETING PLACES Cafeteria in the Pavilion.

DISTANCES IN MILES Montréal, QC 38; Ottawa, ON 115; Québec City, QC 192.

Mont Blanc

Located an hour and a half north of Montréal, Mont Blanc is the Laurentian's best kept secret. Established in 1957, this ski area has since doubled in size by joining facilities with neighboring Mont Faustin. With a new mountain completed in 1991, its skiable terrain is now 36 runs.

Skiing is primarily beginner and intermediate, with a few black diamond bump runs. For boarders, there's an awesome park with a 325-foot half pipe. On-slope, beginners should head for the Yodel while skiers looking to cruise should try the Slalom. Experts start out on the Couloir and work up to skiing or riding the Cougar, Mont Blanc's signature double diamond. If you're looking for variety, Mont Blanc has teamed up with Mont Habitant and Gray Rocks for the Laurentian Tri-Area Season Pass, and offers a selection of terrain comparable to Laurentian giant, Tremblant.

MONT BLANC	
CENTRAL LINE	819-688-2444 or 450-476-1862
CENTRAL RESERVATION LINE	800-567-6715
SNOW REPORT	819-688-2444
ANNUAL SNOWFALL	150 inches.
INFORMATION	www.ski-mont-blanc.com
SEASON	Late Nov — mid-April.
HOURS	Daily, 8:30 am — 4 pm.

The ski school offers individual and small group lessons from one to four hours. For those who want a day off, the sports complex has an indoor pool, hot tubs, and a steam and sauna room. The resort also has daycare for two- to six-year-olds. Call 800-567-6715 for reservations.

Kids ages two to ten love the indoor playground. One of the biggest and best of its kind, the huge labyrinth of slides, pools of balls, tunnels, bridges and tightropes captivate young ones all day long. Children can also play in the recreational room or go for a sleigh ride. Evening entertainment includes activities such as magic shows, bingo, piñata parties and casino nights. Overnight guests can night ski at Mont Habitant, 40 minutes south on Highway 15. Or, go snow tubing nearby with Les Aventures Neige (819-429-5500).

Mont Blanc has ski-in ski-out lodging with a country-style setting and spacious fully equipped condos. Call (800-567-6715) to reserve. Guests generally book year after year due to the resort's quality, convenience and excellent value.

👁 At a Glance

ADDRESS 1006 Route 117, Saint-Faustin-Lac-Carré, Québec J0T IJ3.

LOCATION Central Québec.

TERRAIN MIX 2 mountains, 150 acres.

VERTICAL 983 feet.

TRAILS 36 (22% Beginner, 30% Advanced, 48% Expert).

LIFTS 7 (2 quads, 2 triples, 1 double, 2 surface).

DAILY LIFT TICKET RATES (CDN) Adults $33, seniors (60 to 69) and youths (13 to 20) $27, children (6 to 12) $20, seniors (over 69) and tots (under 6) $5.

SNOWMAKING 85%.

NIGHT SKIING None.

ACTIVITIES Sleigh rides, bingo, casino nights, magicians, swimming, sauna, cross-country, snowmobiling, La Jungle Magique (playroom with giant maze, slides, Tarzan swing and ball pits).

BABYSITTERS Call to reserve (800-567-6715).

DAYCARE Daily, 8:30 am—4 pm, 2 to 6 years (819-688-2444).

CHILDREN'S LESSONS AND CAMPS Ski & Snowboard School (800-567-6715).

HOSPITAL Centre Hospitalier Laurentien (819-324-4000).

SPECIAL DEALS Family Special (with purchase of Adult full-day ticket, child gets reduced price), Ladies' Day (Tuesdays) Men's Day (Wednesdays).

GOOD MEETING PLACES La Jungle Magique.

DISTANCES IN MILES Montréal, QC 70; Ottawa, ON 150; Québec, QC 225.

Mont Tremblant

Situated just 90 minutes from Montréal in the Laurentian mountains, Mont Tremblant is one of the continent's earliest ski areas and has become one of the best. In 1991, mega-resort operator Intrawest bought the resort and invested $800 million in its development. The results are spectacular—an award-winning village, snowmaking on 80 percent of the terrain, more runs, plus plenty for families.

Start by visiting the Kidz Club that operates beside Tremblant's base area Snow School (88-TREMBLANT or 819-681-5666). Youngsters (ages one to six) can join the Mother Nature Daycare (819-681-5666). Older kids can partake in a wide range of classes. Tremblant is one of a handful of resorts that offers traditional ski weeks with 14 hours of lessons spread over seven days with the same instructor. Classes include video analysis, friendly races and group pictures ($160 per week). If you have beginners over 13, try out the Magic Trax program that serves up group lessons, rentals and a lift ticket for $59. Instructors speak English and French.

Just outside the base area there's a conveniently located magic carpet. For a lengthy beginner slope, try Nansen that winds down the southern face. Kids should keep their eyes open for Tremblant's numerous Adventure Parks, such as the Enchanted Forest and Couloir des Algonquins off the La Passe green run. Intermediates can cruise on Beauvallon, while snowboarders hit the Gravity Snow Park located on the north side. Experts should pick up a map and check out the mountain's amazing steeps, gladed terrain and black diamond runs.

MONT TREMBLANT
CENTRAL LINE 819-681-2000 or 88-TREMBLANT
CENTRAL RESERVATION LINE 800-461-8711
SNOW REPORT 819-681-2000
ANNUAL SNOWFALL 150 inches.
INFORMATION www.tremblant.ca
SEASON mid-Nov—mid-April.
HOURS Daily, 8:30 am—3:30 pm (until 4:15 pm after Dec 21st). Wed and Sat, 6:30 pm to 10 pm.

Off-slope, try the groomed Nordic ski trails at the Tremblant Adventure Center. There's also horseback riding, dog sledding and tubing. Or visit the art gallery, relax with a spa treatment at Chateau Mont Tremblant or head to the library and pick out some great books. Pack your bathing suits and take the kids to Aquaclub La Source. This wet and wild facility comes complete with an indoor tropical pool and open-air hot tub. For more ideas, call or visit the Activity Center in Place St. Bernard (819-681-4848).

For shopping and dining, Place St. Bernard (the pedestrian village) has over 75 Québec-style boutiques and restaurants. Sit in one of the cafés and enjoy a cold drink, coffee or pastry while you watch skiers carve down the slopes. On Wednesday and Saturday nights from 6:30 pm to 10 pm, Tremblant lights up the Flying Mile so that skiers and boarders can strut their stuff. The resort plans special activities for kids (5 to 12) on Sunday and Tuesday evenings.

Need more excitement? Visit the website (www.tremblant.ca) or call (819-681-3000 ext. 46261) to find out what event is taking place the week you plan to visit. For accommodations, there's a huge selection, from the five-star Fairmont Tremblant to the St. Bernard condo suites. Call (800-567-6760) to see what's best for your family's budget.

From World Cup freestyle to terrain park parties and more, Tremblant serves up an irresistible blend of French Canadian joie de vivre, European charm and first-class amenities.

◉ At a Glance

ADDRESS   3005 chemin Principal, Mont Tremblant, Québec J0T 1Z0.
LOCATION   South central Québec.
TERRAIN MIX   1 mountain, 610 acres.
VERTICAL   2,131 feet (**PEAK** 3,001 feet. **BASE** 870 feet).
TRAILS   92 (17% Beginner, 32% Intermediate, 40% Advanced, 11% Expert).
LIFTS   12 (an 8-person high-speed gondola, a 6-person high-speed gondola, 5 high-speed quads, 1 quad, 3 triples, 1 magic carpet).
DAILY LIFT TICKET RATES (CDN)   Adults $54, seniors (65 to 79) and youths (13 to 17) $40, children (6 to 12) $30, over 79 and under 6 free.
SNOWMAKING   65%.
NIGHT SKIING   1 lift, Flying Mile trail.
ACTIVITIES   Kids' Nights (Sat and Tue) Welcome cocktail for kids (Mon), tubing (Wed), Aquaclub (indoor and outdoor pools, hot tubs, wading pool and tarzan rope) movies, Nordic skiing, dog sledding, horseback riding, ice climbing, snowmobiling, snowshoeing, Scandinavian baths, spa, sleigh rides.
BABYSITTERS   Contact Day Care (819-681-5666).
DAYCARE   Mother Nature's Day Care, daily, 8:30 am—4:30 pm, 1 to 6 years (819-681-5666).
CHILDREN'S LESSONS AND CAMPS   Kidz Club (819-681-5666), Ski Camp for teens.
HOSPITAL   Ste-Agathe des Monts Hospital (819-324-4000).
SPECIAL DEALS   Busy Parents Season Pass (joint pass for 2 adults), Student Pass, visit www.tremblant.ca for more deals.
SPECIAL PROGRAMS   Ladies Get-Away, Mountain For All, First Tracks.
GOOD MEETING PLACES   Le Grand Manitou Rest Area (peak), Information Desk (Place St. Bernard).
GETTING AROUND   Free shuttle bus to parking lots.
DISTANCES IN MILES   Boston, MA 385; Montréal, QC 90; New York, NY 450; Toronto, ON 390.

EASTERN TOWNSHIPS

Owl's Head

Just an hour and a half southeast of Montréal on the western shore of Lake Memphremagog, Owl's Head is the fourth highest ski peak in eastern Canada (after Le Massif, Mont-Sainte-Anne and Tremblant) and one of the most scenic. Despite its 86 acres of terrain and 36 marked trails, this family-run resort is still relatively unknown. Expect a warm, family-style retreat instead of the glitz and glamour common elsewhere. Anyone skiing here will soon realize that Owl's Head offers the best skiers/riders-to-ski-acres ratios in the region.

On-slope, beginners cruise mild trails such as Winkler or Nice & Easy, while intermediates choose Porc-Epic and the scenic Upward Trail. There are a handful of snaking expert runs and five double diamonds for those who want to take the plunge. Snowboarders and new school riders have Panorama terrain park and half pipe cachet all to themselves. Looking for a scenic way down? Set your edges on Lily's Leap and revel in the kaleidoscope panorama of the Eastern Townships.

Owl's Head Ski and Board School is one of the most underrated in the country. Sign up for a reasonably priced ($90) week-long package, complete with 10 hours of group lessons, video sessions and fun races with your group. Newbies can join the Iniski program and get full rentals, lift ticket and a one-hour lesson—all for $30. Inisurf for boarders only costs $40. Daycare for two- to five-year-olds operates out of the Main Lodge. To reserve in advance for daycare or Iniski and Inisurf programs contact (450-292-3342).

OWL'S HEAD

CENTRAL LINE
450-292-3342

CENTRAL RESERVATION LINE
800-363-3342

SNOW REPORT
800-363-3342

ANNUAL SNOWFALL
145 inches.

INFORMATION
www.owlshead.com

SEASON
Mid-Dec—mid-April.

HOURS
Daily, 8:30 am—4 pm.

There is more to Owl's Head than just the slopes. Spend the afternoon strolling through the quaint town of Knowlton, only a short drive away. Perfect for window-shopping, the old time streets are filled with first-class restaurants, great novelty shops, designer boutiques and a theater.

Overnight guests can choose from simple hotel rooms at Auberge Owl's Head, to one, two or three bedroom condos with full kitchens and fireplaces at the Owl's Head Apartment/Hotel. All accommodations at Owl's Head are slope-side and provide ski-in and ski-out access. Remember to bring some games, as nighttime is typically quiet at Owl's Head. Guests can drop in for a casual Monday night wine and cheese get-together, or join in the Karaoke nights held Wednesday in the Owl's Head Bar.

👁 At a Glance

ADDRESS P.O. Box 35, Mansonville, QC J0E 1X0.
LOCATION Southeastern Québec.
TERRAIN MIX 2 mountain peaks, 86 acres.
VERTICAL 1772 feet (**PEAK** 2480 feet. **BASE** 708 feet).
TRAILS 36 (36% Beginner, 33% Advanced, 31% Expert).
DAILY LIFT TICKET RATES (CDN) Adults $32, students (over 14 with ID) $25, children (6 to 13) $20, seniors (65 to 69) $10, seniors (over 69) $5, under 6 free.
SNOWMAKING 90%.
NIGHT SKIING None.
ACTIVITIES Nordic skiing, tubing, ice-skating.
BABYSITTERS Call (450-292-3342).
DAYCARE Owl's Head Drop-In Centre, daily, 8.30 am—4 pm, 2 to 5 years (450-292-3342).
CHILDREN'S LESSONS AND CAMPS Owl's Head Ski & Board School (450-292-3342).
HOSPITAL La Providence Hospital (819-843-3381).
SPECIAL DEALS Skiing & Lodging packages, visit www.owlshead.com for details.
GOOD MEETING PLACES Base Lodge Cafeteria.
DISTANCES IN MILES Albany, NY 220; Boston, MA 247; Montréal, QC 99; Ottawa, ON 206; Sherbrooke, QC 49.

QUÉBEC CITY

Mont-Sainte-Anne

You can't beat Québec City's winter charm—or the size and scale of its largest lift-accessed mountain. Enjoy Québec's renowned joie de vivre at Mont-Sainte-Anne, located three-and-a-half hours east of Montréal and a half-hour from the historic Québec City waterfront. It's a great spot to spend a weekend or weeklong family trip.

The resort offers great discounts and value for families. There are three free lifts (one is a magic carpet) that access family-friendly slopes dotted with figurines and fun features. Once your youngsters can ski down beginner runs by themselves, head over to Enchanted Forest. Located on the north side of the mountain, this gladed trail was specially designed for children with animal figure cutouts and the great wooded atmosphere kids love. Afterwards, bring the family to the La Familiale green run, or the intermediate, La Pichard. There's also a mid-mountain sugar shack where you can indulge in "la tire" and other timeless maple syrup specialty products from Québec.

MONT-SAINTE-ANNE
CENTRAL LINE
418-827-4561
CENTRAL RESERVATION LINE
800-463-1568
or 418-827-5281
SNOW REPORT
888-827-4579
ANNUAL SNOWFALL
160 inches.
INFORMATION
www.mont-sainte-anne.com
SEASON
Mid-Nov—early May.
HOURS
Daily, 9 am—10 pm (opens at 8:30 am on weekends).

New to the resort? Get acquainted with the complimentary ski tours held daily at 10 am and 1 pm. If backcountry skiing interests you, check out the West Side's terrain—it's likely you'll discover untouched snow. The resort's 56 trails are spread over 430 skiable acres, so it's easy to find a trail that suits your ability. Looking from atop, expert runs are on the right, intermediate in the middle and beginner terrain on the left. Experts like to carve up the "S" and "Super S," while intermediates cruise the top-to-bottom Gros Vallon. Snowboarders and new age skiers enjoy the terrain parks and two half pipes off La Grande Allee.

Sainte-Anne's Planet Snow was rated one of the top ski schools in the country, and covers every detail from an efficient check in to creative lesson planning. All services for children are available under one roof, which makes it easier for parents and fun for kids who "graduate" from one area to another. It includes a nursery (ages 6 to 18 months) and features amenities younger children need, including nap room with cribs and high chairs for meals. Daycare (418-827-4561 ext. 341) also welcomes older children (up to 12 years) and offers a variety of activities, from singing and dancing to handicraft, cooking and fun games in the center's park. Planet Snow offers very popular Adventure Ski and Ride camps for more active kids and all instructors are bilingual.

Non-skiers can skate on the ice rink (rentals available), dog sled, snowmobile, sleigh ride, horseback ride, or paraglide. Mont-Sainte-Anne has the largest cross-country ski facility in Canada (418-827-4561 ext. 408). There are numerous slope-side restaurants and several ski bars, which offer live music and après-ski like nowhere else—make sure to check out Jazz Nights at the Chouette Bar every Friday. Other nighttime activities include eating crêpes near the base of the gondola, night skiing seven days a week and snowshoeing (Tuesday night package includes a night of snowshoeing and a fondue dinner). Call the Snow Activity line at 888-827-4579 or 418-827-4579.

There is almost unlimited slope-side accommodation available with many different lodging facilities to choose from. Les Chalets Montmorency is a popular retreat for families or large groups (800-463-2612 or 418-826-2600). Call the central reservation number (800-463-1568) for more information on local hotels and condos. No matter when you go or where you stay, you'll experience Québec hospitality and skiing at an affordable price.

◉ At a Glance

ADDRESS   2000 boulevard Beaupré, P.O. Box 400, Beaupré, QC G0A 1E0.
LOCATION   Québec City.
TERRAIN MIX   1 mountain (3 faces), 428 acres.
VERTICAL   2,050 feet (**PEAK** 2,625 feet. **BASE** 575 feet).
TRAILS   56 (23% Beginner, 46% Advanced, 18% Expert, 13% Extreme).
LIFTS   13 (an 8-passenger gondola, 3 high-speed quads, 1 quad, 1 triple, 2 doubles, 5 surface, 1 magic carpet).

DAILY LIFT TICKET RATES (CDN) Adults $42.60, seniors (over 64) and youths (14 to 22) $34.80, children (7 to 13) $25, under 7 free.

NIGHT LIFT TICKET RATES (CDN) Adults $19.10, seniors (over 64) and youths (14 to 22) $16.50, under 7 free.

SNOWMAKING 80%.

NIGHT SKIING 4 lifts, 15 trails, 2,050 feet vertical.

ACTIVITIES Sleigh riding, ice-skating, snowshoeing and fondue dinners (Tue), dog sledding, paragliding, snowmobiling.

BABYSITTERS Check with your hotel concierge.

DAYCARE Children Center, daily, 8:30 am — 4 pm, 6 months to 10 years (418-827-4561 ext. 341).

CHILDREN'S LESSONS AND CAMPS Children Center (418-827-4561 ext. 341).

HOSPITAL Clinique Médecine de Famille (418-688-1385).

SPECIAL DEALS 5-day pass includes free Nordic skiing and access to Le Massif and Stoneham.

SPECIAL PROGRAMS Program for the Disabled, Iniski and Inisnow (lift ticket, equipment rental and lesson) Mont-Sainte-Anne Ski Week (personalized 4-day program with video sessions).

GOOD MEETING PLACES Côté Jardin (Base Lodge), Rond Point (Summit Lodge).

GETTING AROUND Bus Shuttle, daily, 8:30 am — 4:30 pm, free.

DISTANCES IN MILES Albany, NY 395; Boston, MA 400; Montréal, QC 180; New York, NY 574; Québec City, QC 25; Toronto, ON 520.

CHAPTER SIX

Eastern United States

From the peaks of Vermont's Green Mountains to the legendary alpine bowls of Sugarloaf in Maine, visitors to New England will find some of the best family ski areas in North America. Because competition among resorts is huge, families can anticipate a host of services and facilities at excellent prices.

Smugglers' Notch leads the pack when it comes to inventive children's programming. Expect everything from skiing mascots to magicians at this family-friendly resort. Tucked away on the other side of Spruce Peak, Stowe is classic mountain getaway. Here, there's a plethora of activities at the award-winning Adventure Center. Other Vermont retreats include the family-run Okemo, lively Stratton and the no-holds-barred Killington, with its six interconnected mountains and over 200 trails to choose from. Families love fun of the non-skiing variety in Mad River Valley near Sugarbush—including Ben & Jerry's™ Ice Cream Factory tours.

New Hampshire skiers have a gem in the mid-sized Waterville Valley. This ski area has an impressive array of family options not available at mega-resorts, including snow toy rentals, free lessons for intermediate and experts, and the exciting tubing park. Moms taking a mid-week break with the kids love the great deals on Women's Wednesdays.

Families looking for that at-home feeling will want to ski at Sugarloaf, on the flanks of Maine's second highest peak. The resort offers terrific programming, from their inviting childcare to the exciting Mouseketeers program for young skiers/riders to the Sugarloaf Extreme Team for teens. Sunday River, located near the New Hampshire border, comes with all the amenities for a memorable family vacation. Bring a camera and snap photos of views of the Presidential Range from Jordan Bowl, and don't miss the Nite Cap Fun Center, hub of family-friendly activities at this resort.

0   50   100   150   200   250 miles

0   50   10   150   20   250   300   350 km

Eastern United States

New Hampshire
★ Waterville Valley

Maine
★ Sugarloaf
★ Sunday River

Vermont
★ Killington
★ Okemo
★ Smugglers' Notch
★ Stowe

NEW HAMPSHIRE

Waterville Valley

W ant to vacation at a moderately-sized resort with lots of services for families? Look no farther than Waterville Valley, ranked by *Ski Magazine* as one of the top five east coast mountains for family programming, lodging and best overall resort.

Part of Waterville Valley's award-winning program, the innovative Snowsports School, offers a wide range of lessons involving new techniques, equipment and snow toys. There are three different age-related programs for kids, an adaptive program for disabled skiers and senior lessons for those over 55. Advanced and expert skiers and boarders are invited to brush up on their skills for free at the resort's refresher lessons held on Mondays and Fridays. Register in advance at the Snowsports desk in the Base Lodge and meet the group at the White Peak Quad at 1:30 pm.

When your crew is ready for snow action, start slowly at Kinderpark and Pasture beginner areas situated close to the base. Intermediates cruise down White Cap and old Tecumseh. True Grit and the Lower Bobby double diamond glades found at the summit are a challenge for even the most experienced skiers. If you're boarding, get some air at The Boneyard or ride the Exhibition half pipe. Mini-snowboarders can strut their stuff at Little Slammer Park.

All season long, you'll have great snow with Waterville Valley's 100 percent snowmaking coverage. Every trail leads back to the base, so parents can let youngsters ski on their own without worrying about them getting lost. Want to meet for lunch?

WATERVILLE VALLEY RESORT

CENTRAL LINE
603-236-8311

CENTRAL RESERVATION LINE
800-GO-VALLEY
(468-2553)

SNOW REPORT
603-236-4144

ANNUAL SNOWFALL
132 inches.

INFORMATION
www.waterville.com

SEASON
Early Nov—late April.

HOURS
Daily, 9 am—3:45 pm
(opens at 8 am on
weekends and holidays).

Try the mid-station Sunnyside Up Restaurant or the base area cafeteria. With accommodations only minutes away, you could head back to the condo and make your own meal.

Waterville Valley also offers great deals for families. Kids 6 to 12 with lift tickets can rent snow toys for free in Exhibition Park, and go tubing every morning until noon (it's also open on weekends and holiday evenings for $8 an hour). On Women's Wednesdays, discounted lessons, free ski toy rental and free childcare are available for moms at the homey, state-licensed facility (603-236-8311 ext. 3196).

Because the mountain is located in the White Mountain National Forest, there are no on-site accommodations available. However, there is a variety of lodging to choose from just two miles away in Waterville Valley Village. For a family favorite, try the Black Bear Lodge (800-349-2327). Its one-bedroom, condo-style units are spacious and can sleep six comfortably. Children enjoy the nightly movie at the family cinema.

The hotel offers guests free access to the White Mountain Athletic Club, just a few steps away. The club has a pool, saunas, steam rooms, racquet sports, weight room, massage room and even an arcade for teens. Traveling in a bigger group? Try the Waterville Valley Town Square (800-GO2-WVTS), which accommodates guests with three-bedroom suites. Hotels offer free shuttle service to Waterville Valley every 20 minutes.

◉ At a Glance

ADDRESS 1 Ski Area Road, P.O. Box 540, Waterville Valley, NH 03215.
LOCATION Central New Hampshire.
TERRAIN MIX 1 mountain, 255 acres.
VERTICAL 2,020 feet (**PEAK** 4,004 feet. **BASE** 1,984 feet).
TRAILS 52 (36% Beginner, 44% Advanced, 20% Expert).
LIFTS 12 (2 high-speed quads, 2 triples, 3 doubles, 4 surface, 1 magic carpet).
DAILY LIFT TICKET RATES (US) Adults $49, seniors (over 64) and youths (13 to 18) $42, children (6 to 12) $19, under 6 free. (Seniors get a discount on weekdays).
SNOWMAKING 100%.
NIGHT SKIING None.
ACTIVITIES Fireworks, teen recreation center, free children's theater at Bear Lodge Resort, free wine and cheese (Sat), dinner under the stars (at Schwendi Hutte) tubing, sleigh rides, moonlight ski tours, ice-skating, Nordic skiing, snowshoeing.
BABYSITTERS Contact front desk at your hotel.

DAYCARE   Waterville Valley Child Care, daily, 8 am—4:30 pm, 6 months to 4 years (603-236-8311 ext. 3196 or 3197).

CHILDREN'S LESSONS AND CAMPS   Snowsports School (603-236-8311 ext. 3136 or 3135).

HOSPITAL   Speare Memorial Hospital (603-536-1120).

SPECIAL DEALS   Women's Wednesdays (free childcare), seniors ski for $19 during the week, check www.waterville.com for seasonal offers.

SPECIAL PROGRAMS   Silver Streaks (55+), Adaptive programs, 3-day Women's Retreat.

GOOD MEETING PLACES   Sunnyside Up Lodge (on-slope), Fireplace (Base Lodge).

GETTING AROUND   Shuttle Bus, daily, 7:30 am—4:30 pm, free.

DISTANCES IN MILES   Boston, MA 130; Manchester, NH 70; Montréal, QC 225; New York, NY 325; Toronto, ON 525.

MAINE

Sugarloaf

In 1951, Sugarloaf opened its doors to skiers who were looking for a friendly, low-key atmosphere to enjoy the snow.
Maine's second highest peak has since experienced plenty of
visitors, but the resort's approach to skiing remains unchanged.
There's not much glitz at this resort, just a laid-back ski environment that families love.

Kids of all ages have an extensive roster
of programming to choose from. Tots (six
weeks to two-and-a half years) can attend
the bright and roomy Sugarloaf/USA Child
Care Center (207-237-6959) located in
Gondola Village. Youngsters intent on learning to ski or board should sign up for the
American Ski Company's Perfect Kids program, which ranges from the Mooseketeers
for three-year-olds, to the Sugarloaf Extreme
Team for ages 13 to 16. Adults wanting to
brush up on their technique can register for
the daily Perfect Turn clinics (800-THE-
LOAF).

Families venturing out on their own
feel comfortable riding any of the base area
chairs, as beginner runs come off each chair.
If you're looking for intermediate terrain, head to the upper
mountain lifts and ski the renowned New England groomers,
King's Landing and Tote Road. Ride the Timberline quad to the
4,237-foot summit for superb 360-degree panoramas and challenging double diamond descents. Skiers and snowboarders can
head to the Superpipe or any of the three terrain parks to get big
air.

Keep an eye out for the resort's four mascots—Amos the
Moose, Pierre the Lumber Jack, Lemon the Yellow Nosed Vole

SUGARLOAF/USA
CENTRAL LINE
207-237-2000
CENTRAL RESERVATION LINE
800-THE-LOAF
(843-5623)
SNOW REPORT
207-237-6808
ANNUAL SNOWFALL
242 inches.
INFORMATION
www.sugarloaf.com
SEASON
Early Nov—early May.
HOURS
Daily, 9 am—3:50 pm
(opens at 8:30 am on
weekends).

and Blueberry the Bear. They often make cameo appearances in the beginner ski areas and are available for birthday parties. Kids enjoy stopping at Amos' cabin off Cruiser run. Moose Alley is just around the corner and offers an alpine playground full of fun and surprises.

Après-ski activity at this lively resort continues with nightly events for kids and families, including movies, game nights, golf clinics, turbo tubing, snowshoe safaris, family adventure suppers and more. For active families wanting a break from alpine skiing, try hockey, ice-skating, sleigh rides, guided tours, cross-country skiing or snowshoeing. Contact the Outdoor Center for more information (207-237-6830). If you'd rather take it easy, peruse the shops in the local village.

For a real taste of New England, enjoy fresh lobster at the Seasons restaurant or a local microbrew at Shipyard Brewhaus, located slope-side at Sugarloaf Inn. Families also enjoy relaxing at the Double Diamond Steakhouse and Pub in the Grand Summit Resort Hotel. Teens hang out at the Avalanche, in the Base Lodge, where they can munch on pizza and other kid-food.

Looking for lodging? Plan to stay at the Grand Summit Resort (800-527-9879 or 207-237-2222). There is also a wide range of off-slope hotels, bed & breakfasts and inns. Call 800-THE-AREA to find the best deals. No matter where you stay, the Valley Shuttle runs free all day and well into the night. There's no need to drive anywhere.

👁 At a Glance

ADDRESS RR 1, Box 5000, Carrabassett Valley, ME 04947-9799.
LOCATION Western Maine.
TERRAIN MIX 1 mountain, 530 acres.
VERTICAL 2,820 feet (**PEAK** 4,237 feet. **BASE** 1,417 feet).
TRAILS 126 (24% Beginner, 28% Advanced, 20% Expert, 18% Double Diamond).
LIFTS 15 (2 high-speed quads, 2 quads, 1 triple, 8 doubles, 1 surface, 1 magic carpet).
DAILY LIFT TICKET RATES (US) Adults $51, youths (13 to 18) $46, seniors (over 64) and children (6 to 12) $33, under 6 free.
SNOWMAKING 92%.
NIGHT SKIING None.
ACTIVITIES Tubing, fireworks, torchlight parades, birthday parties with mascots, Teen Club, Nordic Skiing, snowshoeing, ice-skating, dog sledding, snowmobiling, sleigh rides, women's non-skiing programs.

BABYSITTERS Call Child Care Center (207-237-6959).
DAYCARE Child Care Center, daily, 8 am—4:30 pm, 6 weeks to 6 years (207-237-6959).
CHILDREN'S LESSONS AND CAMPS Perfect Kids (207-237-6924).
HOSPITAL Franklin Memorial Hospital (800-398-6031).
SPECIAL DEALS check www.sugarloaf.com for seasonal deals.
SPECIAL PROGRAMS Family Theme weeks, Avalanche Center for teens, Women's Ski Clinics.
GOOD MEETING PLACES King Pine Room (base).
GETTING AROUND Sugarloaf Shuttle, daily, 8 am—midnight, free.
DISTANCES IN MILES Boston, MA 230; Montréal, QC 180; Portland, ME 130.

Sunday River

With eight snow-filled peaks, Sunday River spreads over three miles and features terrain parks, myriad family-friendly beginner and intermediate trails, three base areas and amusing off-slope activities. Sunday River is also at the forefront of the adaptive ski program, run by the Maine Handicapped Ski operation (207-639-7770).

Most families begin their day at the South Ridge Base Lodge and Welcome Center. Drop the tots off at the licensed daycare (207-834-5081), or bring your young skiers to the Perfect Kids learn-to-ski program. Interested in some ski tips for yourself? Check the Perfect Turn Discovery Center (207-834-5078) and have top instructors teach you to carve in style.

Just outside the South Ridge Lodge, there are plenty of green runs, including the Who-ville™ terrain park and mini pipe, and an award-winning network of lifts. Beginners don't need to restrict themselves to this base—every chair (except the Locke Mountain triple) has an easy way down. Boarders flock to the super pipe and terrain parks, while experts venture to White Cap peak for thrilling steeps. Intermediate

SUNDAY RIVER SKI RESORT

CENTRAL LINE
207-824-3000

CENTRAL RESERVATION LINE
800-543-2SKI (754)

SNOW REPORT
207-824-5200

ANNUAL SNOWFALL
155 inches.

INFORMATION
www.sundayriver.com

SEASON
Early Nov—early May.

HOURS
Daily, 9 am—4 pm (opens at 8 am weekends and holidays).

slopes make up 40 percent of Sunday River's terrain, so families have plenty of suitable runs. For picture-perfect views, check out the panorama of Mount Washington and the Presidential Range from atop Jordan Bowl.

When the sun goes down, head to the White Cap Base Lodge, home to the Nite Cap Fun Center. There's family dining at Rossetto's, live music at Bumps! Pub, expansive night-lit tubing areas, arcade, ice-skating and bonfires. Be sure to catch the fireworks on Thursday and Saturday nights. If you need more action, visit the nearby town of Bethel. It has a movie theater, sleigh rides (207-824-2595) and The Ultimate Big Adventure Center (207-824-0929) with laser tag and rock climbing walls.

Slope-side, families should stay at the Grand Summit Resort Hotel & Conference Center. This first-class facility includes a spa, fitness center, outdoor pool and hot tub. There are plenty of other options—call 800-543-2SKI for more information.

Sunday River hasn't finished growing yet. The foundations have been laid for developing the exclusive Jordan Village. The improvement project includes a huge pedestrian village with retail shops, restaurants, private home sites and luxury condominiums. Expect more great quality and friendly service.

👁 At a Glance

ADDRESS P.O. Box 450, Bethel, ME 04217.

LOCATION Western Maine.

TERRAIN MIX 8 mountains, 654 acres.

VERTICAL 2,340 feet (**PEAK** 3,140 feet. **BASE** 800 feet).

TRAILS 127 (25% Beginner, 35% Advanced, 40% Expert).

LIFTS 18 (4 high-speed quads, 5 quads, 4 triples, 2 doubles, 3 surface).

DAILY LIFT TICKET RATES (US) Adults $51, seniors (over 64) and children (6 to 12) $33, under 6 free.

SNOWMAKING 92%.

NIGHT SKIING None.

ACTIVITIES Tubing, sledding, fireworks, family theater and concerts at the Grand Summit Resort Hotel, Health Club, massages, Snowcat rides, Nordic skiing, White Cap Fun Center, snowshoeing.

BABYSITTERS Hotels will provide list of referrals.

DAYCARE Grand Summit Daycare, daily, 8 am—4:30 pm, 6 weeks to 6 years (207-824-5889). Jordan Grand Daycare (207-824-5314). South Ridge Day Care (207-824-5083).

CHILDREN'S LESSONS AND CAMPS Perfect Turn Ski & Snowboard School (207-824-5081).

HOSPITAL Western Mountain Clinic (207-824-5262). Bethel Family Health Center (207-824-2193).

SPECIAL DEALS Visit www.sundayriver.com for seasonal deals.

SPECIAL PROGRAMS Prime Time Club (50+ group activities), Black Diamond Club (weekend ski group for intermediate and advanced skiers), Women's Turn clinics, Maine Handicapped Skiing.

GOOD MEETING PLACES North Peak Lodge, Shipyard Brewhaus (Barker Base Lodge).

GETTING AROUND Sunday River Trolley, daily, morning through evening, free.

DISTANCES IN MILES Bethel Airport, ME 6; Boston, MA 180; Montréal, QC 235; New York, NY 384; Portland, ME 75.

VERMONT

Killington

Boasting six interconnected mountains and only a short bus ride from Pico, Killington is the biggest, highest, best all-around resort on the east coast. Its 32 lifts shuttle you up to the slopes earlier and stay open later than any other resort in the region. And no matter how early or late you choose to ski, Killington's snow (more snow-making than any other resort on the planet) is money-back guaranteed!

When you come to test out the terrain, go to Ram's Head, Killington's first stop for ski families. Pick up your lift tickets, rental equipment, lunch and snacks. Ram's Head makes it easy for families to unload, with a 15-minute parking area at the door. The base is designed for kids—phones are knee high and small-sized gear fills the mini-lockers. Even the restrooms are kid-sized and the restaurant offers affordable daily specials. Just outside, the slopes are family-oriented with patrollers enforcing speed control.

The Friendly Penguin Nursery and Day Care Center (800-621-MTNS), and Killington's Perfect Kids program are based at Ram's Head. The daycare rooms overflow with toys for tots, while the ski school breaks down into First Tracks (2 to 3), Ministars and Lowriders (4 to 6) and Superstars (7 to 12). Families can choose between full day (including lunch) and half-day programs. The Magic Carpet conveyor belt lift is monitored by animators, who help kids turn on their skis. Youngsters descend with locked-together ski tips, until they are able to stop.

Teens head to SnowZone, Killington's new Perfect Turn program upstairs in the Loft. In this program, young adults choose

---

KILLINGTON MOUNTAIN RESORT

CENTRAL LINE
802-422-3261

CENTRAL RESERVATION LINE
800-432-0100

SNOW REPORT
802-422-3261

ANNUAL SNOWFALL
250 inches.

INFORMATION
www.killington.com

SEASON
Oct—June.

HOURS
Daily, 9 am—4 pm (opens at 8 am on weekends).

a clinic by deciding which zone—tree skiing, snowboarding the steeps, racing, ski-boarding stunts in the terrain parks and boarder/skier cross—they want to conquer. The Loft also doubles as a teen hang out.

For older beginners, Snowshed's Family Center and novice ski area lie just across the street, under the ski bridge from Ram's Head. It includes a learning area with poma lift and three chairlifts that service wide-open slopes. Six restaurants operate at Snowshed's Family Center, but box lunches are also welcome. Mom and Dad can check out the après-ski action at the Long Trail pub, while kids enjoy the music and ambience in the family rooms next door. On the main level, Green Mountain Climbing Center's rock wall can warm up frozen-toed skiers (three climbs for ten dollars). If you're awaiting your youngster's arrival from ski school, relax in the Perfect Turn Discovery Center private lounge, annexed onto Snowshed and decked out with sofas by the fireplace, complementary fruit, donuts and hot chocolate.

When ski school is out, strut your stuff on Killington's half pipe and three terrain parks, some of the best in the East. If you want a break from your boards, throttle down the Ground Zero Tubing Park. It's open from noon to 6 pm every day (Wednesdays and Saturdays until 9 pm). Bring the kids and their skates too, as Ground Zero operates an adjacent ice rink and outdoor fireplace. Saturdays are family nights at Snowshed with free face painting, an inflatable Baboon Typhoon jumping game and movies. On Saturday nights, teens head to Bumps, Killington's only under-21 dance club where local DJs spin the latest tunes until midnight.

Killington also offers Family Ski Week Adventures during the height of the season. Enjoy the parties, ice cream socials, snowshoeing, horse-drawn sleigh rides, family fun races and flag parades. Kids' Night Out enables parents to spend a quiet evening while kids delight in supervised activities. The ski week closes with a farewell party and sends everyone home laughing, after watching video footage of the family slalom race.

Although it's biggest in the East, Killington hasn't stopped growing. Watch for the proposed Pico connection, which will link the two mountains. Since Killington's superlatives do cost, price savvy families may want to look for deals in Pico. Part of the Killington Family, Pico comes with 48 trails, 7 lifts, its own terrain park, and a base village with children's center. There's also a learning area separate from the rest of the hill. For details, call

Killington's main reservation line (800-621-MTNS) or log onto www.killington.com.

👁 At a Glance

ADDRESS   Killington Road, Killington, VT 05751.

LOCATION   Central Vermont.

VERTICAL   3,150 feet (**PEAK** 4,241 feet. **BASE** 1,091 feet).

TERRAIN MIX   7 mountains, 1,160 acres.

TRAILS   200 (30% Beginner, 39% Intermediate, 31% Expert).

LIFTS   32 (2 gondolas, 6 high-speed quads, 6 quads, 6 triples, 4 doubles, 7 surface, 1 magic carpet)

DAILY TICKETS RATES (US)   Adults $58, students with ID $53, seniors and children $36, under 6 ski free. Pico Mountain only: Adults $45, students with ID $35, seniors and children $20, under 6 free.

SNOWMAKING   70%.

NIGHT SKIING   Ground Zero Fun Park has a half pipe open during the evening.

ACTIVITIES   Family Fun Night (tubing, climbing wall, dinner), snowmobile tours, tubing, ice-skating, cross-country skiing, snowshoeing, indoor rock climbing, horse-drawn sleigh rides, spa, Ram's Head Family Center activities.

BABYSITTERS   Friendly Penguin (802-733-1330).

DAYCARE   Friendly Penguin DayCare, 6 weeks to 6 years (800-621-MTNS).

CHILDREN'S LESSONS AND CAMPS   Perfect Kids (802-422-3333).

HOSPITAL   Rutland Medical Center (802-775-7111).

SPECIAL DEALS   Under 13 ski free with purchase of adult 5-day pass, Canadian Week (CDN at par), Super Saver (pre- and post-season lift and lodging deals).

GOOD MEETING PLACES   Ram's Head or Snowshed base.

GETTING AROUND   Skibus, daily, 8 am—5 pm (starts at 7 am on weekends).

DISTANCE IN MILES   Albany, NY 120; Burlington, VT 80; Montréal, QC 190; New York City, NY 270; Ottawa, ON 300.

Okemo

Do kids in your family like big air? Be sure to add Okemo to your list of must-ski destinations. This family-owned resort caters especially to teens, with some of the most innovative terrain parks in the East—including a 420-foot Super Pipe. Add excellent pricing, an abundance of intermediate terrain, seasonal specials and 95 percent snowmaking coverage, and you've got a classic Vermont vacation that everyone will love.

Make your first stop the Cutting Edge Learning Center. Here you can sign up for one or more of Okemo's lesson options, from women's clinics to Ski Stars for tots to Park and Pipe snowboard classes. Once you've registered, drop your kids off anytime after 7:45 am on weekends. Sessions begin at 9 am and end at either 11:30 am for half-day, or 3 pm for full-day lessons. If you've got non-skiers (ages six weeks to eight years), the licensed Penguin Playground is conveniently located in the base lodge. Pagers are offered for a nominal fee, and there's an optional Kid's Night Out from 6 pm to 10 pm on Saturdays.

Not sure you're going to like the snow? Guest Services offer a "Try Before You Buy" program where the first hour of skiing is free. Once you've warmed up on the beginner trails, head to the sprawling blue runs. It's easy to see why Okemo has been ranked number one in the East for the past three years in the groomed trail category. Want an even better deal? Kids under seven ski or ride for free, all season long.

OKEMO MOUNTAIN RESORT
CENTRAL LINE
802-228-4041
CENTRAL RESERVATION LINE
800-78-OKEMO (65366)
SNOW REPORT
802-228-5222
ANNUAL SNOWFALL
200 inches.
INFORMATION
www.okemo.com
SEASON
Early Nov—late April.
HOURS
Daily, 9 am—4 pm (opens at 8 am on weekends and holidays).

If you'd like a complimentary tour of the mountain, meet the blue-jacketed ambassadors at 10 am at the Sugar House Lodge. Hungry for lunch? Head to the Solitude Base Lodge for a quiet family meal. The atmosphere is hard to beat and so is the restaurant's famous soup!

Once you've stowed your skis for the day, hit some balls at the Okemo Valley Indoor Golf Academy. Contact the Nordic Center (800-228-1396) for snowshoeing or cross-country skiing fun. If you'd rather go fast, try snowmobiling (802-228-2870). For something more relaxing, Okemo's village offers plenty of shopping and dining facilities. Kids get a kick out of the knick-knacks at Vermont Country Store.

To round off the amazing value, Okemo's selection of luxury slope-side condos offers free accommodation to kids under 13. Call 800-78-OKEMO for reservations and information. Current improvements to the resort are underway, including Jackson Gore Mountain Village and 30 percent more terrain. This is one resort experience that families won't want to miss.

👁 At a Glance

ADDRESS 77 Okemo Ridge Road, Ludlow, VT 05149.

LOCATION South central Vermont.

TERRAIN MIX 2 mountains, 520 acres.

VERTICAL 2,150 feet (**PEAK** 3,344 feet. **BASE** 1,194 feet).

TRAILS 98 (25% Beginner, 50% Advanced, 25% Expert).

LIFTS 14 (3 high-speed quads, 4 quads, 3 triples, 3 surface, 1 magic carpet).

DAILY LIFT TICKET RATES (US) Adults $56, seniors (65 to 69) and youths (13 to 18) $48, seniors (over 69) and children (7 to 12) $36, under 7 free.

SNOWMAKING 95%.

NIGHT SKIING None.

ACTIVITIES Kids' Night Out (pizza, movies), sleigh rides, Nordic skiing, snowshoeing, ice-skating, virtual golf at Okemo Valley Nordic Center, spa, health club, swimming pool, snowmobiling.

BABYSITTERS Contact Penguin Playground (802-228-1554).

DAYCARE Penguin Playground Day Care Center, daily, 8 am — 4:30 pm, 6 weeks to 8 years (802-228-1554).

CHILDREN'S LESSONS AND CAMPS Cutting Edge Learning Center (802-228-4041), Get Altitude Adventure Clinics (teens).

HOSPITAL Okemo Regional Medical Center (802-228-4666).

SPECIAL DEALS first hour lift operations is free, Okemo Flex Card (discounts on weekdays and weekends), Okemo 8-Pack (8 days of skiing for the price of 7), Discounts on Thursdays for residents of selected states, visit www.okemo.com for deal details.

SPECIAL PROGRAMS Women's Ski Spree, Early Tracks, Parent and Tot Lessons, Adaptive Instruction, Snow Tracks (learn about the wildlife and nature of Okemo) Create-Your-Own Lesson.

GOOD MEETING PLACES Summit Lodge (Northstar Express Quad), Base Lodge Café, Sugar House Lodge (Northstar Express Quad).

GETTING AROUND Village Shuttle, service on weekends and holiday periods, 7:30 am — 6:30 pm, free. Resort Shuttle Service, daily, 9 am — 4 pm, free.

DISTANCES IN MILES Albany, NY 92; Boston, MA 232; Hartford, CT 135; New York, NY 248, Ottawa, ON 290; Philadelphia, PA 340.

Smugglers' Notch

S mugglers' ranks high in the family category in most ski and mountain resort magazine polls. The reason is simple —Smugglers' knows how to have family fun. Kids of all ages love to ski and snowboard at this resort. Morse Mountain has tows made for kids—two slow-speed, near to the ground, doubles with mid-station off-loading points, and Handle tow in Sir Henry's Fun Park, which doubles as a tubing center and beginners' snow-boarding venue.

New skiers head to Morse Highlands Lodge and its lifts, which rise 375 vertical feet and service 22 acres of beginner trails. The Lodge has its own interactive museum with a Four Seasons of Vermont Forests theme, where you can learn about logging, sugaring-off and local wildlife while warming up. Just outside is the Wanderer Nature Trail, where kids stop off for hot chocolate and conversation in the Tee Pee (Thursdays and Saturdays).

SMUGGLERS' NOTCH
CENTRAL LINE
800-451-8752
or 802-644-8851
CENTRAL RESERVATION LINE
800-451-8752
SNOW REPORT
802-644-1111
ANNUAL SNOWFALL
272 inches.
INFORMATION
www.smuggs.com
SEASON
Late Nov—mid-April.
HOURS
Daily, 8:30 am—4 pm.

Whether you bring infants or tots, childcare is second to none. Youngsters (6 weeks to 3 years) head over to Alice's Wonderland (800-451-8752), a state of the art, million-dollar facility. Bigger kids venture to the Discovery Center, which bustles with daylong skiing and non-ski activities. Advanced children and teens can join the many ski/boarding daily programs. Rest assured your kids are in good hands—day-care and ski school programs come with all the amenities and a full lunch. On-slope programs end at 3 pm, but movies or live science shows—Smugglers' integrates science into all part of its kids' programs—will captivate young minds until 4 pm.

If you're here to ski, don't let the family designation mislead you. Smugglers' 67 trails snake down northern Vermont's biggest vertical drop at 2,610 feet. Boarders and new school skiers have their own surface lift up to Prohibition Park's half pipe. Madonna Mountain has the first and only triple diamond trail in the East—The Black Hole at Freefall Woods. Carve up the forest at

Smugglers' infamous glades—some of the best in the country. Its double chairs are sluggish compared to modern high-speed quads, but that just gives you a break between thigh-burning runs.

At day's end, meet the kids with a change of clothes at the 3:30 pm daily bonfire with Smugglers' mascots Mogul Mouse, Billy Bob Bear and Frostie the Snowmaker. Grab a hot chocolate and walk around Smuggs' Central. Children love the FunZone —an inflatable building behind the pool. Inside there are basket-ball, hockey, inflatable obstacle course races, and even a two-story high adrenaline-pumping slide. Enjoy golfing? Check out the nine-hole indoor mini-putt. Don't forget to bring your swimsuit. The indoor pool and hot tub are open from 10 am to 9 pm. On your way back to the condo, visit the goats, sheep and other furry creatures at the petting zoo.

If you're skiing with teens, expect them to disappear to their own après-ski hangout—the Yurt. Every day of the week (7 pm and 9 pm), there are special events for young adults. On Saturday night, teens take over the FunZone for a thumping DJ dance (complete with big screen movies and inflatable games) that lasts from 9 pm until midnight.

Lodging is a stone's throw away from Smuggs' Central and once parked, you can forget about your car. Most condos have VCRs, TVs and CD/Stereos. Try the two-bedroom lodging at Sycamore. Bedrooms come with a double and two single beds. Kitchens are fully equipped, and the Village Grocery Store has all the extras, including video rentals. If you're tired of cooking, there are five restaurants in Smugglers' Village and two pubs at Madonna/Sterling.

How about booking a nighttime getaway? Try a romantic evening's snowshoe atop Sterling summit, complete with candle-lit dinner. Call Alice's Wonderland for their night care programs (which include kid-friendly dinners) and babysitters.

Smugglers' aim is to please families. And they know how to do it—their Snow Sports University programs are money-back guaranteed. The only sad faces you'll see will be yours and your children's when it's time to leave.

👁 At a Glance

ADDRESS 4323 Vermont Route 108 S., Smugglers' Notch, VT 05464-9537.
LOCATION Northern Vermont.
VERTICAL 2,610 feet (**PEAK** 3,640 feet. **BASE** 1,030 feet).
TERRAIN MIX 3 mountains, 260 acres.
TRAILS 67 (22% Beginner, 53% Advanced, 19% Expert, 6% Extreme Expert).
LIFTS 9 (6 doubles, 3 surface).
DAILY LIFT TICKETS RATES (US) Adults $48, youths (7 to 18) $34, over 69 and under 6 free (rates may increase slightly during holiday season).
SNOWMAKING 60%.
NIGHT SKIING None.
ACTIVITIES Snowmobiling, snowshoeing, tubing, FunZone, Tub Club Spa, family movies, Parents' Night Out, family karaoke, bingo, games night, outdoor ice-skating, Outer Limits Teen Club, Nordic Ski & Snowshoe Treks.
BABYSITTERS Alice's Wonderland, reservations required (802-644-1180).
DAYCARE Alice's Wonderland (802-644-1180).
CHILDREN'S LESSONS AND CAMPS Snow Sports University (800-451-8752).
HOSPITAL Cambridge Regional Health Center (802-644-5114).
SPECIAL DEALS Club Smuggler's Packages saves 30% off many activities (800-451-8752).
SPECIAL PROGRAMS Nature education programs, Boy Scout badge-earning program, recreational racing, 55-Plus Club, Study Hall (supervised by certified teachers).
GOOD MEETING PLACES The Gazebo (Morse base), FunZone.
DISTANCE IN MILES Albany, NY 180; Burlington, VT 30; Montréal, QC 93; New York, NY 360; Ottawa, ON 205.

Stowe

S towe is northern Vermont's classic ski resort. It offers an unforgettable alpine experience: 480 skiable acres spread over three mountain peaks, a lively base area, and an excellent Children's Adventure Center, all covered with 272 inches of white stuff every winter.

Bring your brood to the Spruce Base Lodge. This is the mountain set aside for beginners and intermediates — complete with a ski school-specific chair (Toll House double). There's a bright and friendly non-ski daycare for children between six weeks to six years old. Children from three to 12 years can join the award-winning Adventure Center. There are teen camps and even Mom and Dad can sign up for instruction. Best of all, everyone has a blast. Stowe boasts one of the best ski school programs in the East—make sure to register early as classes fill quickly. Call the Welcome Center to make reservations for daycare and ski school (802-253-3000).

STOWE MOUNTAIN RESORT	
CENTRAL LINE	
800-253-4SKI (754) or 802-253-3000	
CENTRAL RESERVATION LINE	
800 253-4SKI (754) or 802-253-3000	
SNOW REPORT	
802-253-3600	
ANNUAL SNOWFALL	
260 inches.	
INFORMATION	
www.stowe.com	
SEASON	
Mid-Nov—late April.	
HOURS	
Daily, 8 am—4 pm (opens at 7:30 am weekends and holidays). Thu—Sat, 5 pm—9 pm.	

Slope-side, beginners can meander down the lengthy 3.7 mile-long Toll Road, while experts carve up slopes atop the Four Runner Quad on Mt. Mansfield, Vermont's highest peak. Nosedive is a great advanced cruiser and National is covered with huge bumps. Intermediates tend to prefer the terrain atop the world's fastest gondola. If you haven't had enough action during the daylight hours, the Gondolier Trail is lit until 9 pm, Thursday to Saturday on midseason nights. Skiers wanting to check out Smugglers' Notch Resort can take a run over via the Connector on Spruce Peak (Stowe guests purchasing a multi-day lift ticket may spend one day at Smugglers' at no extra charge).

Families can partake in a range of off-slope activities such as snowshoeing, cross-country skiing or going for a horse-drawn sleigh ride at the world famous Trapp Family Lodge (802-253-8511). If you want solitude, there's over 150 miles of groomed and 100 miles of untracked Nordic trails. For information about backcountry snowmobiling, call Stowe Snowmobile Tours (802-253-6221). In town, you can shop at factory outlets, eat at one of the numerous restaurants or see what's playing at the Stowe Cinema 3-Plex (802-253-4678).

There is a limited amount of on-site accommodation, but the selection is excellent. Try the Inn At The Mountain & Condominiums (800-253-4SKI), or stay at the Hob Nob Inn (hotel rooms and rustic cabins, 802-253-8549). Watch for the new village going up over the coming years. This $200 million project will launch new base lodge facilities, as well as a National Park-styled luxury hotel.

◉ At a Glance

ADDRESS   Mt. Mansfield Co. Inc, 5781 Mountain Road, Stowe, VT 05672-4890.

LOCATION   Northern Vermont.

TERRAIN MIX   3 mountains, 480 acres.

VERTICAL   2,360 feet (**PEAK** 4,395 feet. **BASE** 1,559 feet).

TRAILS   48 (16% Beginner, 59% Advanced, 25% Expert).

LIFTS   11 (an 8-person high-speed gondola, 1 high-speed quad, 1 triple, 6 doubles, 2 surface).

DAILY LIFT TICKET RATES (US)   Adults $56, seniors (over 64) and children (6 to 12) $35, under 6 free.

NIGHT LIFT TICKET RATES (US)   Adults $20, seniors (over 64) and children (6 to 12) $16, under 6 free.

SNOWMAKING   73%.

NIGHT SKIING   Gondola lift line.

ACTIVITIES   Ice-skating, movie theater, library activities, Nordic skiing, sleigh rides, snowmobiling, snowshoeing.

BABYSITTERS   Contact Children's Adventure Center (802-253-3000).

DAYCARE   Cub's Daycare, daily, 8 am — 4:30 pm, 6 weeks to 6 years (802-253-3000).

CHILDREN'S LESSONS AND CAMPS   Children's Adventure Center (802-253-3000).

HOSPITAL   Copley Hospital (802-888-4231).

SPECIAL DEALS   Ski and lodging packages.

SPECIAL PROGRAMS   Teen Adventure (socially-oriented program for intermediate and advanced teens), Demo/Learn Program (personal coaching while demo-ing latest ski and board models).

GOOD MEETING PLACES   Cliff House Restaurant (top of gondola), Easy Street Café (Spruce Base Lodge), Mansfield Café (Mansfield Base Lodge).

GETTING AROUND   Inter-Mountain Shuttle, during ski hours, free. Village/Mountain Trolley, 8 am — 9 pm, $1.

DISTANCES IN MILES   Boston, MA 205; Burlington Airport, VT 40; Montréal, QC 140; New York, NY 325.

Glossary

Alpine skiing   Downhill skiing. Generally refers to using skis with bindings that fix hard-shelled boots rigidly to the ski. Skier uses a pair of poles for balance and uses gravity to travel down slopes.

Après-ski   Social activity after a day of skiing.

Backcountry skiing   Any kind of skiing done away from developed land or open roads.

Basket   A round disc near the bottom of a ski pole that prevents the shaft from sinking into the snow.

Berm   A terrain park feature people use to get airborne.

Bindings   Automatic mechanisms that attach boots to skis. Protect skiers from potential injury during a fall by releasing skis from boots.

Black diamond   An expert trail demarcated by a black diamond on a white background.

Blue square   An intermediate trail demarcated by a blue square on a white background.

Board(s)   Slang for snowboard and skis.

Bowl   An open mountain area shaped like a bowl, usually without trail boundaries. Generally advanced or expert terrain.

Brake   A stopping device on ski bindings that prevents a loose ski from sliding down the hill.

Bump(s)   Moguls. Mounds or lumps of snow that can either be formed naturally or created by skiers.

Bunny run   A beginner trail.

Carve   When you turn in an arc by shifting your weight onto the edge of your skis or snowboard.

Chairlift   The most common type of ski lift. It carries skiers on chairs that hang from a moving cable.

Christie   A beginner turn that combines wedge and parallel styles.

Chute   A narrow run usually bordered by rocks, for experts only.

Cross-country skiing   Nordic skiing. Generally refers to using a diagonal stride while wearing soft boots and bindings that clip at the toe and leave the heel loose. It is characterized, for most skiers, by a walking action (opposite arm/opposite leg motion), which evolves into a stride and glide (known as classic or traditional technique). Ski skating or "freestyle" technique combines a double polling action of arms with a speed skating-like leg motion and relies on decisive weight shift to propel the skier forward.

Cruiser   A wide, groomed slope usually of intermediate level.

DIN (Deutsche Industrial Norm)   A release measurement taken for ski bindings that takes size, age and skier ability into consideration.

Double diamond   A very difficult expert trail, demarcated by two black diamonds on a white background.

Downhill skiing   *see* Alpine skiing.

Edges   The metal sides of skis and snowboards.

Express chair   A high-speed detachable chair that carries three, four or six people.

Fall line   The gravitational line down the hill (for example, the trajectory water would take down a slope).

Glade   A skiable, wooded area. Usually advanced or expert terrain.

Gondola   A ski lift with enclosed cabins (two to ten people) which people ride while holding their skis/snowboards.

Green circle   A beginner trail, demarcated by a green circle on a white background.

Groomed terrain   A trail or slope that has been smoothed over by a machine.

Half pipe   U-shaped terrain feature popular with snowboarders and new age skiers.

Hit   A terrain feature that gets riders airborne.

Kicker   A raised area with a lip that snowboarders use to launch themselves into the air.

Leash   A clip that ties snowboard to snowboarder.

Magic carpet   A beginner's lift that functions like a moving sidewalk.

Moguls   Bumps. Mounds or lumps of snow that can either be formed naturally or created by skiers.

Monoski   A long, wide ski that looks like a snowboard but with traditional ski bindings so the rider faces completely forward.

Nordic skiing   *see* Cross-country skiing.

Parabolic   Hourglass-shaped skis designed for enhanced carving and control.

Parallel   An advanced form of skiing performed by keeping skis equidistant from each other.

Patroller   A trained medical specialist who skis or snowboards at resorts and is available for medical emergencies (also Ski Patroller).

Pipe dragon   A machine that shapes and grooms half pipes.

Platter lift   A one-person surface lift.

Poma lift   A surface lift that runs on a cable with a disc-shaped "seat" that riders place between their legs and it pulls them up the hill.

Powder   Fresh, deep, light snow with low moisture content that has not been compacted.

Rail(s)   A thin, long terrain park feature made of metal or plastic for riders to do balancing tricks.

Side-slipping   A slipping motion straight down the fall line with skis pointed across the hill.

Skiboarding   Using two "snowboard-shaped" skis that are less than three feet long.

Spine   A long, triangular-shaped berm found in terrain parks.

Shussing   Skiing at a fast speed.

Six-pack   A high-speed chairlift for six people.

Snowcat   A snow vehicle with caterpillar tracks used to groom snow or transport skiers.

Snowboard   A board like a wide ski ridden in a surfing position downhill over snow.

Snow making   A system of blowing pressurized water onto slopes to create artificial snow.

Snowplow   A beginner technique to control speed, turning and stopping by making a wedge with skis. The front tips of the skies almost touch, while the back tips are bowed outward.

Surface lift   A lift where riders never leave the ground.

T-bar   A surface lift that pushes two skiers uphill at a time. It is shaped like an upside down "T," where the bar tucks behind a skier's thighs.

Tree line   A line above which trees cannot grow.

Tabletop   A mound of snow with a flat surface on which snowboarders can land or jump over.

Telemarking   A cross between alpine and cross–country skiing. Requires special equipment. It typically involves one ski slid forward and a distinctive forward bent knee position while turning.

Terrain park   Area popular with snowboarders that contains berms, pipes and special features designed for jumps and tricks.

Torchlight dinner   An evening activity including a mountaintop meal and a flashlight descent.

Trail markings   The symbols that indicate the difficulty of a mountain's slopes. Green circles are easiest, blue squares are moderate or intermediate and black diamonds are advanced. A double black diamond indicates the most difficult terrain. (Remember that designations of difficulty will differ from mountain to mountain).

Tram   Large enclosed container lift that skiers ride while holding their skis/snowboards.

Traversing   Continuously moving in a direction across the fall line.

Tuck   To be in a high-speed racing position, bent over with elbows near knees.

Twin tips   Skis with tips on both front and back, enabling rider to ski, jump and land in both directions.

Wedge   *see* snowplow.

Resort Activities and Amenities Chart

	BABYSITTING	DAYCARE	BEGINNER-ONLY TERRAIN	PROGRAMS FOR KIDS	PROGRAMS FOR TEENS	NIGHT SKIING	SNOWBOARDER-FRIENDLY	FAMILY SKI ZONE	DOG SLEDDING	HELI-SKIING	HORSEBACK RIDING	ICE FISHING	ICE-SKATING	NORDIC SKIING	SKE-COLOGY	SLEIGH RIDES	SNOWCAT SKIING	SNOWMOBILING	SNOWSHOEING
WESTERN CANADA																			
Banff Mount Norquay		■	■	■		■	■												
Lake Louise		■	■				■		■	■			■	■		■			
Sunshine Village	■	■	■	■			■												
Fernie	■	■		■	■		■			■			■	■		■		■	
Kimberley	■	■	■	■		■	■	■					■	■		■		■	■
Big White	■	■	■	■		■	■		■	■			■	■		■			
Silver Star	■	■	■	■	■	■	■		■				■	■		■			
Sun Peaks	■	■		■			■						■	■				■	■
Whistler-Blackcomb	■	■		■	■	■	■		■	■			■	■		■			■
NORTHERN ROCKIES AND UTAH																			
Big Sky	■	■		■	■		■				■		■	■		■	■	■	■
Grand Targhee	■	■	■	■			■		■			■	■	■		■	■	■	■
Jackson Hole		■	■	■	■		■		■					■	■	■		■	■
Sun Valley	■	■	■	■			■							■		■			
Alta	■	■	■	■											■				
Brian Head	■	■		■		■	■							■			■	■	■
Brighton & Solitude	■		■			■	■							■					
Deer Valley	■	■	■				■	■	■	■			■	■				■	
Snowbird	■	■	■	■		■								■	■				

158   RESORT ACTIVITIES AND AMENITIES CHART

		BABYSITTING	DAYCARE	BEGINNER-ONLY TERRAIN	PROGRAMS FOR KIDS	PROGRAMS FOR TEENS	NIGHT SKIING	SNOWBOARDER-FRIENDLY	FAMILY SKI ZONE	DOG SLEDDING	HELI-SKIING	HORSEBACK RIDING	ICE FISHING	ICE-SKATING	NORDIC SKIING	SKE-COLOGY	SLEIGH RIDES	SNOWCAT SKIING	SNOWMOBILING	SNOWSHOEING
COLORADO AND NEW MEXICO	Aspen & Snowmass	■	■	■	■	■		■		■				■	■		■	■	■	■
	Beaver Creek & Vail	■	■	■	■	■		■						■	■				■	■
	Copper Mountain	■	■	■	■			■	■					■	■		■		■	■
	Crested Butte	■	■	■				■		■		■		■			■		■	■
	Durango	■	■	■	■			■							■		■	■	■	■
	Steamboat		■		■	■		■					■	■	■		■		■	
	Telluride	■	■	■	■	■	■	■		■	■	■		■	■		■		■	■
	Winter Park	■	■		■			■		■					■		■	■	■	■
	Taos Ski Valley		■	■	■									■	■					■
WESTERN UNITED STATES	Mt. Rose				■			■											■	
	Big Bear & Snow Summit				■		■	■												■
	Kirkwood	■	■		■			■		■			■	■	■		■		■	■
	Mammoth	■	■		■			■		■	■			■	■		■		■	■
	Northstar	■	■	■	■		■	■	■	■	■				■		■		■	■
	Squaw Valley	■	■		■		■	■	■						■		■		■	■
	Mt. Bachelor		■	■	■			■		■					■		■		■	■
	Timberline	■			■		■	■												
	White Pass	■	■		■		■	■						■	■					■
EASTERN CANADA	Mont Habitant		■	■	■	■	■	■						■						
	Mont Blanc		■	■	■										■		■	■		
	Mont Tremblant	■	■		■	■	■	■		■		■			■		■		■	■
	Owl's Head	■	■	■	■			■						■	■					
	Mont-Sainte-Anne	■	■		■		■	■	■	■		■		■	■		■		■	■
EASTERN UNITED STATES	Waterville Valley	■	■	■	■			■						■	■		■			■
	Sugarloaf	■	■	■	■	■		■		■				■	■		■			■
	Sunday River	■	■		■			■							■			■		■
	Killington	■	■	■	■	■	■	■						■	■		■		■	■
	Okemo	■	■		■	■		■						■	■				■	■
	Smugglers' Notch	■	■		■	■									■				■	■
	Stowe	■	■	■	■	■	■	■						■	■		■		■	■

Index

Notes

Notes

Notes

Notes

Notes

The Lobster Kids'
City Explorers series

The Lobster Kids' City Explorers contain
over 150 fun-filled suggestions for family
outings. Each guide is overflowing with great
ideas for all seasons and activities, from simple
family afternoons to all-out birthday parties
and school field trips.

All $17.95 CAN / $12.95 US.
Trade paperback. 232 – 272 pages.

The authors come from a wide variety of
backgrounds. From being moms and dads of
their own broods, they are also published
writers, editors, social workers, children's
entertainers and all-around great explorers.

The City Explorers in the U.S.A.

The Lobster Kids' Guide to Exploring Boston
Deirdre Wilson
1-894222-41-5

The Lobster Kids' Guide to Exploring Chicago
Ed Avis
1-894222-40-7

The Lobster Kids' Guide to Exploring Las Vegas
Heidi Knapp Rinella
1-894222-29-6

The Lobster Kids' Guide to Exploring San Francisco
David Cole and Mary Lee Trees Cole
1-894222-28-8

The Lobster Kids' Guide to Exploring Seattle
Shelley Arenas
and Cheryl Murfin Bond
1-894222-27-X

Lobster Press™

The City Explorers in Canada

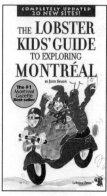

The Lobster Kids' Guide to Exploring Calgary
Kate Zimmermann
and Diane Thuna
1-894222-08-3

The Lobster Kids' Guide to Exploring Montréal
(2nd edition)
John Symon
1-894222-09-1

The Lobster Kids' Guide to Exploring Ottawa-Hull
John Symon
1-894222-01-6

The Lobster Kids' Guide to Exploring Toronto
Natalie Ann Comeau
1-894222-07-5

The Lobster Kids' Guide to Exploring Vancouver
Jeni Wright
1-894222-05-9

Lobster's Family Vacation Series
Upcoming for Fall 2002

Lobster's Family Guide to Cruises
By Veronica Cruz